FEMINISM, OBJECTIVITY AND ECONOMICS

Economics is gender-biased in its definition, methods and models. The emphasis on questions of choice and markets, on the use of mathematical methods, and on models based on individual, rational action reflect a way of conceptualizing the world which has a distinctly masculine slant.

Julie Nelson extends feminist analysis of the influence of masculine norms on the development of Western science, by scholars such as Evelyn Fox Keller and Sandra Harding, to the specific case of economics. As well as evaluating the abstract core models of neoclassical economics, this book includes case studies on topics including the theory of the family, income tax policy and macroeconomics. However, the book does not simply berate economists for the discipline's failings; alternatives such as discarding all current economic practice, or setting up an economics solely for women or for 'women's issues,' are explicitly and emphatically rejected. Rather, it presents the outlines of a less gender-biased discipline which would be richer, more useful and more objective. Such a discipline, informed by feminist theory, would be an improved one, for all practitioners and all subjects.

While in most disciplines the feminist critique is well advanced, this is the first full-length, single-authored book to focus on gender bias in contemporary economics. Its author is a practising academic economist and a leader in the recent development of feminist economics.

Julie A. Nelson is Associate Professor of Economics at the University of California, Davis and Brandeis University. She was joint editor of *Beyond Economic Man* (University of Chicago Press, 1993) and has published widely in leading economics and feminist journals, including *Econometrica* and *Hypatia*.

ECONOMICS AS SOCIAL THEORY
Series edited by Tony Lawson
University of Cambridge

Social theory is experiencing something of a revival within economics. Critical analyses of the particular nature of the subject matter of social studies and of the types of method, categories and modes of explanation that can legitimately be endorsed for the scientific study of social objects, are re-emerging. Economists are again addressing such issues as the relationship between agency and structure, between the economy and the rest of society, and between inquirer and the object of inquiry. There is renewed interest in elaborating basic categories such as causation, competition, culture, discrimination, evolution, money, need, order, organization, power, probability, process, rationality, technology, time, truth, uncertainty and value, etc.

The objective for this series is to facilitate this revival further. In contemporary economics the label 'theory' has been appropriated by a group that confines itself to largely a-social, a-historical, mathematical 'modelling'. *Economics as Social Theory* thus reclaims the 'theory' label, offering a platform for alternative, rigorous, but broader and more critical conceptions of theorizing.

FEMINISM, OBJECTIVITY AND ECONOMICS

Julie A. Nelson

London and New York

First published 1996
by Routledge
11 New Fetter Lane, London EC4P 4EE

Simultaneously published in the USA and Canada
by Routledge
29 West 35th Street, New York, NY 10001

Typeset in Garamond by Datix International Limited, Bungay, Suffolk

Printed and bound in Great Britain by
TJ Press (Padstow) Ltd, Padstow, Cornwall

British Library Cataloguing in Publication Data

A catalogue record for this book is available from the British Library

Library of Congress Cataloguing in Publication Data

Nelson, Julie A., 1956–
Feminism, objectivity and economics / Julie A. Nelson.
p. cm.—— (Economics as social theory)
Includes bibliographical references and index.
ISBN 0–415–13336–X. — ISBN 0–415–13337–8
1. Feminist economics.   2. Economics—Sociological aspects.
3. Sex discrimination against women—Economic aspects.   I. Title.
II. Series.
HQ1381.N45   1994
306.3—dc20
95–21629
CIP

ISBN 0–415–13336–X (hbk)
ISBN 0–415–13337–8 (pbk)

To Anne and Patrick

CONTENTS

ACKNOWLEDGMENTS

I am grateful to many people for helpful discussion of draft chapters and subject areas: Iule Aslaksen, Drue Barker, Allison Berry, Severin Borenstein, Torunn Bragstad, Jürgen Backhaus, Greg Clark, Brian Cooper, Paula England, Marianne Ferber, Diane Felmlee, Nancy Folbre, Sandra Harding, Daniel Hausman, Kevin Hoover, Evelyn Fox Keller, Kathy Kling, Peter Lindert, Linda Lucas, Tom Mayer, Donald McCloskey, Judith Newton, Robert Pollak, Janet Seiz, Amartya Sen, Linda Shaffer, Steve Sheffrin, Stephanie Shields, Evelyn Silvia, Diana Strassmann, Myra Strober, and Frances Woolley. The views of this book should not, of course, be attributed to any of these individuals. I include thanks for comments from (mostly friendly) adversaries.

I also benefited greatly from discussions at several seminars and conferences where I have presented my work. These included presentations for The Center for the Study of Institutions and Values and the Women's Studies Program at Rice University, USA (1989); the Faculty Women's Research Support Group at the University of California, Davis, USA (1989); The Political Economy Club, Harvard University, USA (1991); the De Economische Emancipatiegevolgen van Belastingervorming (Emancipatory Economics and Tax Reform) conference, Rijksuniversiteit Limburg, The Netherlands, (1991); the plenary session on "Women and Economics" at the Canadian Economic Association meetings in Kingston, Ontario, Canada (1991); the Beyond Economic Man conference in St. Louis, USA (1990); the Program in Ethics in Society, Stanford University, USA (1993); the Economics Department at the University of California, Riverside, USA (1993); the "Out of the Margin: Feminist Perspectives on Economic Theory" conference, Amsterdam, The Netherlands (1993); the University of California, Davis, Agricultural Economics Department (1994); and at sessions of the American Economic Association (1989, 1992, 1994), Southern Economic Association (1990), and the International Association for Feminist Economics (1992, 1993, 1994, 1995). I thank Diana Strassmann, Evelyn Silvia, Juliet Schor, Jürgen Backhaus, Martha MacDonald, Linda Lucas, John DuPre,

ACKNOWLEDGMENTS

Stephen Cullenberg, Edith Kuiper, Jolande Sap, Constance Newman, Robert Pollak, Jean Shackleford, Barbara Bergmann and Zoreh Emami, in particular, for their efforts in organizing these fora. I also thank Constance Newman for research assistance. Chapter 6 is based upon work supported by the National Science Foundation under Award No. SES–8921634.

Parts of this book have been excerpted from previously published work, and are printed here with permission. Chapters 1 to 4 include excerpts from "Thinking About Gender," *Hypatia: A Journal of Feminist Philosophy*, Summer 1992, 7(3), 138–54; "Gender, Metaphor and the Definition of Economics," *Economics and Philosophy*, Spring 1992, 8, 103–25 (© 1992 Cambridge University Press); "The Study of Choice or the Study of Provisioning? Gender and the Definition of Economics" in *Beyond Economic Man: Feminist Theory and Economics*, ed. Marianne A. Ferber and Julie A. Nelson, Chicago: University of Chicago Press, 1993 (© 1993 University of Chicago, all rights reserved); and "Value-Free or Valueless? Notes on the Pursuit of Detachment in Economics," *History of Political Economy*, Spring 1993, 25(1), 121–45. Chapter 5 draws from "I, Thou, and Them: Capabilities, Altruism and Norms in the Economics of Marriage," *American Economic Review*, May 1994, 84(2), 126–31. Chapter 6 largely reproduces "Household Equivalence Scales: Theory vs. Policy?" *Journal of Labor Economics*, July 1993, 11(3), 471–93 (© 1993 University of Chicago, all rights reserved). Chapter 7 is an updated version of "Tax Reform and Feminist Theory in the United States Context: Incorporating Human Connection," *Journal of Economic Studies*, 1991, 18(5/6), 11–29. Chapter 9 includes excerpts from "Gender, Metaphor, and the Definition of Economics (*Economics and Philosophy*, 1992), "Gender and Economic Ideologies," *Review of Social Economy*, Fall 1993, 51(3), 287–301 and "On Gendered Economics: Rejoinder," *Review of Social Economy*, 1995, 53(1). Chapter 10 includes excerpts from "Thinking About Gender," *Hypatia*, 1992 and "More Thinking About Gender: Reply," *Hypatia: A Journal of Feminist Philosophy*, Winter 1994, 9(1), 199–205.

INTRODUCTION

This book is about the gender of the discipline of economics. The mainstream academic and professional discipline of economics, as currently practiced in Europe and North America, is built around distinctly masculine-biased notions of what is valuable. My proposal for a remedy, however, is not simply that there should be more women economists (although that would be a good thing). Nor is it that there should be more research on women's issues (although that would be good, too). It is definitely not that women as a class do, or should do, economics in a manner different from men (a position with which I disagree). What is needed to overcome the masculine biases of the profession is a richer conception of human understanding and human identity. These less biased conceptions would broaden and improve the field of economics for both female and male practitioners, and for research on all issues.

Drawing on feminist scholarship regarding the social construction of gender categories and the social construction of science and the academic disciplines, Part I of this book examines the relationship between cultural conceptions of gender and value and the central defining features of contemporary mainstream economics. *Gender*, in this book, is primarily analyzed in terms of how it structures our cognition: that is, how the distinction masculine/feminine is metaphorically related to long lists of other characteristics and qualities. The culturally dominant conception of gender distinctions as hierarchical, with "masculine" on top, leads to high value being attributed to subjects and methods perceived as masculine, and a parallel devaluing of subjects and methods metaphorically associated with femininity. Science, for example, is associated with qualities like "hard" and "tough" (and masculine), in contrast to (inferior) feminine-associated qualities like "soft" or "emotional." Chapter 1 explores the cognitive base of such thinking, and presents a tool, called a "gender-value compass," for thinking about the relation of gender to value in a new way. This simple diagram allows for us to think of masculine- and feminine-associated qualities as having both positive and negative aspects. One can see, for example, that a too enthusiastic quest for "hardness" in science may lead to the vice of rigidity, just as the recognition of appropriate forms of "softness" can lead to the virtue of flexibility. Particularly important for the arguments of this book, it is also noted how the usual emphasis on defining human identity via individuality for men, versus via relationships for women, leads to distortions in the cognitive and ethical, as well as social, realms.

The second chapter notes how this hierarchical gender metaphor has shaped the discipline of economics, and how a more sophisticated way of thinking about gender and value could lead to beneficial transformations of the discipline in subject matter and in method. The current definition of economics is characterized by prototype and by a table of dualisms which outline what is considered to be core subject matter and method, and what is considered to be marginal. The study of markets and the use of mathematical models of individual self-interest, for example, are at the core of the academic discipline, while the study of families and the use of verbal models of social structure and other interest are considered as, at best, barely within the realm of economics. While many economists would take this definition as self-evident and even beneficial, feminist theory about the sources and dangers of masculine bias in science can be brought to bear on this definition of economics. If effort is put into keeping a discipline *masculine* rather than keeping a discipline *good* (i.e., reliable, useful), so that feminine-associated strengths are foregone, masculine-associated weaknesses are allowed to run rampant. Because these notions of gender are culture-wide, the warping of economics in such a gendered fashion is not seen as a conscious act by contemporary, individually malicious, male researchers, but rather as an outgrowth of socially shared cognitive weaknesses. Thinking about what a gender-unbiased definition of economics might look like, and how methods and notions of the "economic agent" would be broadened, constitute much of the subject matter of this chapter.

Chapter 3 explores further how the introduction of feminism, rather than making economics less objective, would make it more objective, by freeing it from one-sided, male-centered assumptions that until recently have gone unquestioned. Current notions of objectivity that value detachment (from the subject, from other researchers, etc.) to an extreme, are seen as themselves culturally constructed and emotionally loaded. The alternative is not radical relativism or subjectivism, but a quest for reliable knowledge that recognizes the role of the knower and that of the context of investigation.

In Part II, the rubber meets the road. These case studies apply the mode of analysis suggested in Part I to specific topics in economics.

While the material in the first three chapters is indispensable for the understanding of the main argument of the book, each case study chapter is fairly self-contained and the chapters in Part II may be read selectively, according to the reader's interest, and in any order. These case studies should all be accessible to both the general reader and the economist, with the possible exception of parts of Chapters 5 and 6 which contain more technical material.

The first case explores the historical development of norms of detachment within the history of economics. The "statements of purpose" of the American Economic Association and the Econometric Society provide interesting texts for studying the changing, and gendered, notions of objectivity in economics over the last century.

Feminists have long been concerned with the treatment of the family in economics. Chapter 5 reviews feminist critiques of the well-known Beckerian model of household behavior, but also adds to this analysis additional examples of masculine bias, an analysis of strengths and weaknesses of recent bargaining models, and concrete suggestions for ways in which the economics of the family might most profitably develop.

The material on household equivalence scales in Chapter 6 was originally published in a mainstream economics journal, without a single reference to gender bias. The economics literature that deals with the question of how to adjust measures of household income for household composition provides, however, a fertile ground for developing a concrete (if lengthy and technical) example of feminist economic analysis. This particular economics literature has developed in such a way that human dependency on others during youth, and on material resources throughout one's life – traditionally, of course, associated with dependency, weakness, and femininity – have become progressively eliminated from economic theorizing and the resulting empirical practice. As a result, theoretical and empirical work in this area has become increasingly detached from the policy question that is, presumably, its rationale.

The U.S. "individual" income tax is the subject of the case study in Chapter 7. The history of the income tax in the U.S.A., and the beliefs about household labor and horizontal equity on which policy has been based, are explored. The U.S. tax structure currently gives a "marriage benefit" to earners who marry homemaker spouses, but puts a "marriage tax" on many two-earner married couples. I suggest that a fairer structure would take as the unit of taxation neither "the household" nor "the individual," but, based on a concept of persons-in-relation, use as the tax unit the individual earner plus his or her economic dependents.

While it may be granted that feminists have something to say about the analysis of the household, economists tend to be much more critical of the idea of feminist improvements when it comes to other areas of economics. Critics, rightfully (if perhaps prematurely) demand to know how a feminist analysis would give a different result in, say, macroeconomics. Chapter 8 examines current controversies in macroeconomics and empirical economics from a feminist perspective, and suggests that, while a feminist analysis does not dictate the results of a study, it radically re-evaluates what we count as reliable knowledge. The growth of "New Classical" macroeconomic methodology, as an example, is examined in light of the cognitive association of abstract, formal models and formal econometric testing with rigor and masculinity. The sad state of empirical economics is argued to be associated with the low status of concrete data work and searches for empirical regularities, each in turn associated with "softness" (and femininity).

The neglect of other topics in this series of case studies should not be construed as conferring on them immunity to critique and improvement, but only the limitations of the author.

The chapters in Part III are replies to various criticisms of this work which have been put forth by economists on the one hand, and feminists on the other. The reader may only want to read one or the other, depending on background and interest. Economists who are familiar with any of the many previous books and articles criticizing mainstream economics might wonder if the feminist work adds anything new to the analysis. Chapter 9 compares and contrasts the feminist analysis presented here with rhetorical, humanistic, and postmodernist critiques of economics. Meanwhile, feminists have divergent views about gender. Some argue for a goal of gender neutrality, others for a "revaluation" of feminine-associated traits, and still others for a postmodernist explosion of dualistic thinking. Chapter 10 argues that the view embedded in the "gender–value compass" of Chapter 1 capitalizes on the strengths of each of these views, while avoiding their weaknesses.

As much of my analysis has to do with the system of values implicit in current mainstream economic practice, I am sometimes asked about the empirical basis of my description of these values. The data on which I base such assertions are of an ethnographic or anthropological nature: I have learned the values by being an economist. My experience as an economist began as a graduate student in economics at the University of Wisconsin, Madison. I have worked at the World Bank and the U.S. Department of Labor, as well as an academic economist. Simultaneously with my feminist and methodological work, I carry on a mainstream research program in the area of empirical demand analysis (and regularly publish in that area in respectable, and sometimes top, journals). My "data" on the values of the profession hence come not just from books or classes, then, but also from seminars, committee meetings, conferences, correspondence with journal editors, and informal (though often highly enlightening) hallway conversations. If I have declined to give item-by-item evidence for each assertion about what the profession values, it is because I expect most economists would agree that most of these cultural values are rather obvious and part of the general atmosphere. My perception that, to date, economists have found feminism a safe subject to ignore is borne out in survey data as well (Albelda 1992).

Part I

THEORY, FEMINIST AND ECONOMIC

1

THINKING ABOUT GENDER AND VALUE

WHAT "GENDER" IS NOT

A frequent popular confusion is to take the word "gender" to mean "about women." This interpretation is misleading on two counts. First of all, women are not the only sexed people in the world. Men are also sexed; it is only because maleness has often been confused with universality that the implications of male sexual identity have been pushed into the background. Second, (except where the substitution of "gender" for "sex" is done because of squeamishness about the latter word's possible connotation of sexual activity) "gender" is now used in much scholarly literature to refer to something different from biological sex. Seeking to distinguish between inborn proclivities and socially created stereotypes, feminists have taken over the term "gender" to refer to the latter. While this book takes a feminist viewpoint, in this chapter the term "gender" will be used in a way that also has much in common with the term's older, linguistic, sense.

In linguistics, gender refers to the way in which many cultures divide words into distinct classes and mark them accordingly. While masculine/feminine are common linguistic genders, other classifications such as inanimate/animate can also form the basis for grammatical gender. That is, the emphasis in this book is on the way in which the masculine/feminine distinction serves as a means of classification undergirding language and thought, rather than how the sex/gender system tends to mold men and women in stereotypical ways. This chapter investigates how gender serves as a cognitive organizer, based on the idea of metaphor as a basic building block of understanding. Without this background, the argument of the next chapter – that current economics is held back by its gender associations – can hardly help but be misunderstood.

This chapter investigates current conceptions of gender, and suggests a way of envisioning gender which does not conflate notions of masculinity and femininity with judgments about worthiness.

3

THE LINGUISTIC BASE

"The essence of metaphor is understanding and experiencing one kind of thing in terms of another," as George Lakoff and Mark Johnson say in their work, *Metaphors We Live By* (1980: 5). According to them, and numerous other researchers in the areas of cognition, philosophy, rhetoric, and linguistics, metaphor is not merely a fancy addition to language, but is instead the fundamental way in which we understand our world and communicate our understanding from one person to another (e.g., Ortony 1979; Grassi 1980, cited in Weinreich-Haste 1986; Margolis 1987; McCloskey 1985). Lakoff and Johnson give many examples of how the language we use reflects metaphorical elaborations of more abstract concepts on the foundation of basic physical experiences. Our perception of "up/down," for example, forms the basis for "good is up, bad is down," "reason is up, emotion is down," "control is up, subjection is down," and "high status is up, low status is down." Richer meanings can be found in more complex metaphors such as "argument is war" (reflected in language like "win," "lose," "defend," "attack"), "argument is a journey" (e.g., "step by step," "arrive at conclusions") or "argument is a building" (e.g., "groundwork," "framework," "construct," "buttress," "fall apart").

These metaphors affect our understanding and our action: for example, if we perceive ourselves as engaged in an argument, how we interpret what we hear and how we respond depends in good part on which metaphor we use. Metaphorical understanding is also culturally variable. For example, there could exist another culture that uses the metaphor "argument is dance" and so uses language of esthetics, style and synchronization. All of the above examples are given by Lakoff and Johnson.[1] Echoes of a similar understanding of cognition and communication can be found in works that speak about cognition in terms of "webs of connection" (C. Keller 1986), "patterning" (Margolis 1987; Wilshire 1989), "cognitive schema" (Bem 1981), Gestalts, or analogies, instead of "metaphor." I will use the word "metaphor" loosely, to mean all these things.

One can gain additional insight into the human mind's way of classifying and understanding by looking at "gender" in the strictly

---

[1] While tracing out an intricate pattern of metaphors based on physical experience, Lakoff and Johnson (1980: 29) base their concept of "embodiment" on experiences of separation and self-containment that feminist scholars could identify as distinctly masculine. They also overlook some possible sexual bases for metaphors (e.g., "up is good", see pages 15, 29) that might appear more readily to a feminist linguist or philosopher. Their analysis of "our" use of metaphor may be easily reinterpreted as an analysis of a distinctly masculine (as well as white, Western, and English-speaking) construction of cognition.

4

linguistic sense. Corbett (1991) explains that gender systems always have a semantic core, that is, some words for which the meaning of the word determines its gender. This includes direct association, as, for example, in Spanish one finds *la mujer* (the woman, feminine) and *el hombre* (the man, masculine). Also included in the semantic core are metaphorical associations, mediated through associations of objects with the sexes through myths and children's stories or by association with the customary occupations of the sexes. For example, while the English language has only pronomial (pronoun) gender, dogs are commonly considered more masculine than cats in English-speaking cultures, perhaps due to images in children's literature. Some words may take their grammatical gender only formally, from morphological (word structure) or phonological (sound structure) rules, having no relation (even metaphorical) to sex (Corbett). In this book, it will be gender in the metaphorical sense that is primarily of interest, though I will go beyond the strictly linguistic sense to include metaphorical associations not reflected in word structure and to include parts of speech other than nouns. I will also use "gender" somewhat more narrowly than in the linguistic sense, in that I will discuss only metaphors built on the male/female distinction. The key point, however, is that the masculine/feminine distinction serves as an organizing pattern in our minds and language.

GENDER AND METAPHOR

I use "gender," then, to refer to the cognitive patterning a culture constructs on the base of actual or perceived differences between males and females. Gender is the metaphorical connection of non-biological phenomena with a bodily experience of biological differentiation.

Bodily sexual difference is clearly a salient part of experience starting in early childhood, in most cultures. Yet one of the major breakthroughs in feminist analysis has been the discovery that many (if not most) of the traits assumed to be "essentially" male or female related, in a biological sense, actually have very strong cultural components. Take, for example, the idea that men are more suited for intellectual work than women. The smaller size of the female brain was taken as scientific proof of intellectual inferiority in the nineteenth century (Bleier 1986). While the lack of connection between size and power has since removed this craniometric argument, the undermining of such supposed biological proofs does not necessarily carry with it a cessation of gender attribution. The cultural salience of the idea of women as less intelligent than men may persist in spite of a lack of supporting theory and even in the face of evidence to the contrary.

To say something has the masculine gender, then, is not to say that it necessarily relates to intrinsic characteristics of actual men, but rather to say that it is cognitively (or metaphorically) associated with the category "man." A male person is biologically masculine; a pair of pants (as on the stick figures that adorn restroom doors) is only metaphorically so. An angular abstract shape may also be understood through the metaphor of masculinity, as contrasted to a curvy abstract shape. Cats are generally considered in contemporary American culture to be more feminine (in disregard of their actual sex), whereas dogs are considered more masculine. The Pythagoreans connected masculinity to odd numbers and femininity to even numbers (Lloyd 1984). In all these cases, the attribution of gender tells us more about how human minds work – about our tendency to organize what we see according to gender – than about any properties inherent in pants, shapes, cats or numbers, or about any of the constraints put on men and women in American (or Pythagorean) society. There is general agreement within a particular culture, at a particular time, in a particular context, about which objects, activities, personality attributes, skills, etc. are perceived to be masculine, which are understood as being feminine, and which are more or less ungendered. As the functioning of gender categories varies historically and cross-culturally, I need to clarify here that when I talk about "our" conceptions of gender I will be referring, with all due apologies to non-Western readers, to dominant conceptions held in the modern Western and English-speaking world. When I refer to "masculine" or "feminine" traits, I do not mean traits that are essentially "more appropriate for" or "more likely found in" persons of one sex or the other, but rather traits that have been culturally, metaphorically gendered.[2]

The dominant conception of gender is as a hierarchical dualism. That is, to the metaphorical connections outlined by Lakoff and Johnson of up-in-center-control-rational we can add "superior" and "masculine," and to the connections of down-out-periphery-submission-emotional we can add "inferior" and "feminine." The traditional, dominant conception of gender can be represented by the following picture:

Masculine (+) | Feminine (-)

That is, masculinity and femininity are construed of largely as opposites, with masculinity claiming the high status side of the line. Discussions about the metaphorical connection of this duality with numerous

---

[2] While it is possible that the association of terms with gender categories is stronger in the thinking of some individuals than in others (Bem 1981), this does not negate the idea that certain associations are culturally dominant. The question of what significance to give to biological difference between the sexes is currently being debated in the feminist literature, as Chapter 10 discusses at more length.

other hierarchical dualisms such as science/nature, mind/body, etc. are endemic in feminist scholarship (e.g., Hartsock 1983: 241; Harding 1986: 23). Tables like the following appear with great frequency, illustrating the metaphorical association of particular traits with gender in post-Enlightenment Western, white, thought:

Masculine	Feminine
reason	emotion
hard	soft
etc.	etc.

The tendency to connect metaphorically behaviors, activities, and attributes with masculinity or femininity extends not only to cultural conceptions of appropriate social roles for women and men, but also far beyond, as in the cat and dog example. To a reader who would question the asymmetry of what I argue is the dominant conception of gender (who would, perhaps, prefer to think of the actual social meaning of gender differences in terms of a more benign complementarity) I need only point out some obvious manifestations of asymmetry in the social domain. Rough "tomboy" girls are socially acceptable and even praised, but woe to the gentle boy who is labeled a "sissy." A woman may wear pants but a man may not wear a skirt. Even fathers who consider themselves feminist may feel much more comfortable taking their daughter to soccer practice, than they would taking their son to ballet. The hierarchical nature of the dualism – the systematic devaluation of females and whatever is metaphorically understood as "feminine" – is what I identify as sexism. Seen in this way, sexism is a cultural and even a cognitive habit, not just an isolated personal trait.

One way of changing the understanding of gender and value might be to assert simply that "feminine is good, too." While one might be able to gain some ground by this route, when looking at the roles played by stereotypically feminine concepts and traits, it sooner or later becomes clear that some of these factors are quite unattractive. If masculine is "strong" and feminine is "weak," who wants to be weak? Another way of challenging the association of masculinity with superiority and femininity with inferiority might be to decide to do away with gender associations entirely. Perhaps we can just talk about good and bad traits, and leave gender out of the discussion. While some may hope for such a case as an ultimate goal, it seems premature to throw away gender categories if they still are actively used as cognitive and social organizers. The line between overcoming gender distinctions and simply suppressing (or, the more psychoanalytic might say, repressing) them is, as will be discussed in Chapter 10, one that can be too easily crossed. I suggest a third alternative, based on a more specific diagnosis of what is wrong with the old hierarchical gender dualism.

THE OLD METAPHOR COLLAPSES CATEGORIES

In contrast to traditional dualistic conceptions, I suggest that opposition is itself only unidimensional in its basis of physical orientation, and not in the realms to which the dualism has been metaphorically applied. For example, "down" is clearly the opposite, negation, or reverse of "up," but "emotional" is not unambiguously an antonym for "rational." One might consider "irrational" to be a better antonym. If we think one-dimensionally and assert that each concept can have only one opposite, then the only way out of this dilemma is to collapse the rational/emotional and rational/irrational comparisons by equating emotion with irrationality (and rationality with lack of emotion). But we do not need to be limited to thinking one-dimensionally. "Irrational" is the opposite of "rational" in that it signifies as lack of the latter; "emotional" might be construed as the opposite of "rational" in the sense of complementarity, i.e., that there is some value to achieving a balance including both capacities. My Webster's dictionary (New Collegiate 1974) allows "complementary" as one definition of "opposite." Dare we use it ourselves in our thinking about gender?

I would like to suggest that we think about "opposition" as encompassing relationships both of lack and of complementarity. I will use the word "difference" to include both these aspects of opposition plus a third concept that I will call "perversion." A concept is a perversion of another if it is similar (not opposite) but different due to distortion, corruption, or degradation. For example, emotionalism, or the tendency to make judgments on purely emotional terms (and hence irrationally), is a perverse use of emotional capacity, just as rationalism, in which all emotion is suppressed, is a perverse use of rationality.

The three different concepts of difference − lack, perversion, and complementarity − can be illustrated with reference to conceptions of masculinity and femininity in Aristotle's biology of sexual difference. In thinking about gender in terms of lack, masculinity is defined by certain attributes, and femininity by their absence. For example, from Aristotle: "The woman is as it were an impotent male, for it is through a certain incapacity that the female is female" (quoted in Lange 1983: 9). Women, according to Aristotle, have less "heat" than men and, accordingly, less soul. This corresponds to a metaphor of "more is up; less is down." A second form of difference is for the negative end to be a perversion of the positive end. Again, from Aristotle: "Whatever does not resemble its parents is already in a way a monster, for in these cases nature has . . . deviated from the generic type. The first beginning of this deviation is when a female is produced" (quoted in C. Keller 1986: 47). The female, though having something in common with the male in origin, is considered to be "deviated," deformed, or distorted. This corresponds to a metaphor of "health is up; sickness is down" or "virtue is up; depravity is down." A third way is for opposites to be conceived of as complements. In the hierarchical dualism, the complementary is always asymmetric: socially constructed femininity or biological femaleness is seen as something of a necessary evil. Aristotle, again: "While the body is from the female, it is the soul that is from the male, for the soul is the reality [substance] of a particular body" (quoted in C. Keller 1986: 49). Both are apparently necessary for procreation, though maleness has the role deemed more important. On a metaphorical level, while "up" is quite literally the reverse of "down," the two belong to the same dimension; without experience of one we can have no conception of the other. Complementarity is, as mentioned, part of the dictionary definition of "opposition."

Feminists would obviously not want simply to reaffirm Aristotle's explanation of the differences between men and women. But the idea of multidimensionality may be helpful. The idea that opposition is not itself unidimensional matters because a richer understanding of multidimensional "difference" can free us from the straitjacket of hierarchical, unidimensional thinking about gender. Experience suggests that metaphors are not immutable; in fact the phenomenon of discovery in science (as well as the power of certain kinds of poetry) has sometimes been attributed to the creation of a new metaphorical association (Ortony 1979). Lakoff and Johnson suggest that "new metaphors have the power to create a new reality" (1980: 45).

A NEW METAPHOR: THE GENDER-VALUE COMPASS

My new metaphor retains gender as a cognitive patterning system; it retains hierarchy in matters of value judgment; it retains opposition. I would argue that these are fundamental categories of thought that must be transformed rather than repressed.[3] What this conception of gender

[3] At least, they are fundamental categories for most present-day, English-speaking Westerners. While one can learn much about the limitations of one's own cognitive structure from cross-cultural comparisons, I am skeptical about whether one can, as an adult, deliberately "rewire" one's own cognitive processing at such a basic level that these categories could be overcome. (See Chapter 10.)

gains over the unidimensional dualism is a radical break of gender categories from value categories, and an explicit exposition of the various meanings of difference. It can be presented in the form of a diagram which may seem deceptively simple: it just separates the masculine–positive and feminine–negative ends of the dominant conception into two separate dimensions: feminine/masculine and positive/negative. I hope that this simplicity will make it immediately useful as a cognitive organizer. The apparent simplicity is deceptive because the jump from one to two dimensions doubles the number of categories involved – increases them from two to four – while tripling the types of relationships that can be represented: from that of poles on one dimension to relationships that are horizontal (which will represent *complementarity*), vertical (which will represent *perversion*), and diagonal (which will represent *lack*). This complexity makes the picture richer than it may first appear.

I will present the mechanics of the diagram first and then illustrate with examples of how it may clarify thinking. Imagine a situation or question that asks for a judgment about human behavior and that has often been answered in gender-oriented ways. Draw the diagram in two dimensions:

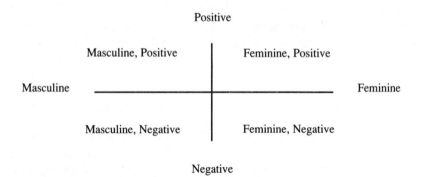

The shape of this diagram should have immediate cognitive "availability" for readers familiar with four-quadrant graphs or two-by-two matrices, without need for further metaphorical elaboration. For those readers who find this diagram unfriendly, I suggest thinking about it as analogous to a directional compass, with poles corresponding to north, south, east, and west. This interpretation suggests further metaphorical insights. As a compass, its service is to guide and direct – in this case to guide our thinking. It also "en*compass*es" a larger space than the old dualistic metaphor, which could be represented by the masculine–positive and feminine–negative diagonal.

The four cells marked off by the axes are related in the following ways. "Good" or positive attributes are entered in the top of the diagram. This obviously involves value judgments. Since this picture is proposed primarily as a template for organizing thinking, it is not absolutely necessary that my "good" and your "good" be the same thing, although the examples to follow unabashedly impose my own judgments. The attributes are marked as masculine or feminine depending on one's judgment of the cultural perceptions regarding the question under study, which again could vary somewhat from person to person as well as vary dramatically from culture to culture. Think of one such concept and put it in the appropriate " + " cell. Opposition in the sense of *lack* is accommodated by putting the term representing the lack of a positive attribute in the negative category under the opposite gender (the diagonal relation). The decision about what attribute reflects "lack" is usually a logical rather than a value-laden or cultural distinction. A negative word representing a *perversion* or distortion of a positive attribute is entered directly below the positive term (the vertical relation, expressing an explicit value judgment). The M + and F + terms should be *complementary* in the sense that one believes that a healthy, balanced behavior involves both traits or activities (the horizontal relationship of positive attributes), while the M − and F − terms may exhibit something of a perverse *complementarity* in that each represents the degenerate form of the corresponding positive trait when its own positive complement is absent (the horizontal relationship of negative attributes). Note that while the relationships of lack and perversion are inherently asymmetric (if we draw arrows in the diagram they point from the top down), this is not true of the relationship of complementarity (which can be illustrated by double-ended arrows):

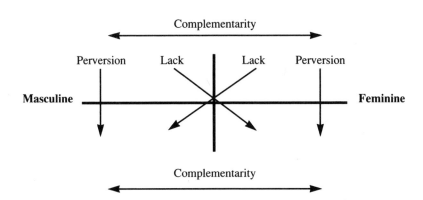

11

The "compass" metaphor for this diagram also highlights the human-defined, culturally variable meaning of gender: objectivity is no more inherently "masculine" than Europe is inherently "Western," though in contemporary discussions of science it often resonates as such. Speaking from an American perspective, it would be more logical, in fact, to say that Europe is "Eastern." Directionality, like gender, depends on the standpoint of the perceiver. Examples of the fluidity of gender categories are legion. Evelyn Fox Keller (1986b) points out that "visibility" is associated with femininity in literary criticism, but with masculinity in the history of science. "Softness" is associated with femininity within a context of white, middle-class culture, but less associated with femininity when images of gender are intermixed with images of race and class. I find it interesting to note that when the image of science under discussion is one of serious, methodical people in white lab coats, creativity is often considered a feminine, flighty attribute. But if the image of science is of a bushy-haired Albert Einstein pondering creative new solutions, it is patience with routine (and the proverbial nimble fingers) that is considered to be the "natural" strength of the feminine gender. From this comes the conclusion that, while women are suited to be laboratory assistants, they are not potential scientists. The point of this diagram is not to set gender–value judgments in stone: it is merely to explore them in their contextual setting when they are culturally salient.

Take as an example the soft/hard distinction given in the simple dualistic chart. The sense in which masculine-associated hardness is good is through its association with strength. The feminine–negative correspondent term, indicating a lack of hardness or strength is "soft," in the sense of "weak." This fills up one diagonal of the diagram:

```
            M+
                        |
                        |
        strong-hard     |
                        |
  ──────────────────────┼──────────────────────
                        |
                        |       F-
                        |
                        |    weak-soft
                        |
```

But hardness can also mean a lack of flexibility, that is, rigidity or a lack of the malleability needed to adapt to changing conditions. "Softness" also has other connotations besides weakness. The aspect of feminine "softness" that needs elevation here is not weakness, but rather flexibility or resilience:

M+	F+
strong-hard	flexible-soft
M-	F-
rigid-hard	weak-soft

Each of the positive terms now in the diagram can be seen as one half of a necessary complementarity to achieve "durability." In addressing a problem, one needs to have the strength to endure at the same time as one needs the flexibility to try new solutions. Weakness is the absence of strength, and rigidity is the absence of flexibility. Weakness is the negative aspect of softness, whereas rigidity is the negative aspect of hardness. The negative complementarity defines "brittleness."

SEPARATION AND CONNECTION IN THE COMPASS

As a more complex example, and one that will undergird many of the later discussions in this book, consider the simple dualistic metaphor of masculine–separate as contrasted to feminine–connected. The relation of gender to the "privileging" of separation and independence, on the one hand, over connection and dependence (or interdependence), on the other, has been traced through history by Susan Bordo (1986) and Sandra Harding (1986); through psychological development by Nancy Chodorow (1980); through personal ethical development by Carol Gilligan (1982, 1986); and through myth and religion by Catherine Keller (1986).

Of these works, the one that has attracted the most popular attention is Gilligan's (1982) work, *In a Different Voice: Psychological Theory and Women's Development*. Prior to Gilligan's work, research into ethical development relied heavily on a model which considered the decision to put rules above relationships as marking an advance in ethical sophistication. It put the conception of ethics in terms of universal principles at the pinnacle of ethical development. Gilligan questioned the notion that there can only be a single path of maturation, and that justice and fairness are exhaustive of sophisticated moral thinking. She suggested that side by side with an "ethic of justice" lies an "ethic of care," that is, an ethic of responsibility towards other persons in relationships. While the justice ethic can be formulated in abstract rules, the care ethic is heavily contextual, and dependent on the recognition of the particular needs of others. Justice is primarily concerned with maintaining fairness among equals; care with maintaining equity and nonviolence among people with different needs and abilities.

Consider, for example, Gilligan's use of the "Heinz dilemma," a brief passage describing the situation of a man who must decide whether to steal a drug that he cannot afford to save his wife's life. According to the justice orientation, this is best seen as the story of a man's decision as to which moral rule (protection of life or of property) logically takes precedence. Yet in interview research some respondents, when faced with this dilemma, tend to go off on what the pre-Gilligan researchers saw as tangents, questioning the morality of the druggist in not donating the drug, for example, or pondering whether Heinz would be able to take care of his wife if he went to jail. While previous researchers had considered these responses to be less mature than those based on abstract principles, Gilligan saw in them a suggestion of a different but equally legitimate interpretation, in which the dilemma is perceived as a story of strained relationships among Heinz, his wife, and the druggist.

Gilligan claimed that in her research the "care" orientation was found to be more typical among women, and the "justice" orientation among men. She in turn related the difference in orientation to the formation of gender identity early in life, drawing on the influential work of Nancy Chodorow (1978). Chodorow argued that girls early on identify with their primary caretaker, since that caretaker is usually a woman, while boys must define their gender identity in opposition to that of their earliest and most intense object of attachment. As a result, she wrote, girls tend to

> define and experience themselves as continuous with others; their experience of self contains more flexible or permeable ego bounda-ries. Boys come to define themselves as more separate and distinct, with a greater sense of rigid ego boundaries and differentiation. The basic feminine sense of self is connected to the world, the basic masculine sense of self is separate.
>
> (Chodorow 1978: 169)

While both these views have been influential in subsequent feminist scholarship, the assertion by Gilligan that the two ethical orientations are sex-linked has been questioned by other feminist scholars (see references in Mansbridge 1993), and agreement among feminists about the validity of Chodorow's psychoanalytic claims is not universal. Some feminists have suggested, for example, that it is not so much distinction between boys and girls as distinction between privileged and less-privileged groups (by race or class as well as sex), that forces some groups into the lesser-valued, identification-by-connection role (Harding 1987).

Unfortunately, the association of connectedness with women in the work of Gilligan and Chodorow tends to reinforce, on the part of the naive observer, the idea that only women are or can be "connected."[4] This has lead, at the mildest, to warnings about the political implications of talking about connectedness (Ruddick 1987); at the most extreme, to the distancing of independence-oriented feminists from feminists involved in the separation/connection conversation, with labeling of the latter as false bearers of the feminist banner. Gilligan's analysis has often been badly paraphrased as saying that "there are two ways of thinking: men's and women's." Books with titles like *Women's Ways of Knowing* (Belenky, *et al.* 1986) may reinforce these views.[5]

It is more helpful, I believe, to focus on how separation and connection have been *culturally and metaphorically* linked with notions of masculinity and femininity. The projection of autonomy on to masculinity and connection to nature and society on to femininity is "embarrassingly empirical," to borrow a phrase from Catherine Keller (1986: 201). Abstract philosophy connects with gendered experience in everyday distinctions between who does the thinking versus who does the dishes; who writes the journal articles versus who writes the Christmas cards; the man who envisages "man" as individual and autonomous versus the woman who changes her name to Mrs John Jones when she marries. What could be a recognition of physical embodiment and social connectedness, as well as individuality, within each person becomes a negative complementarity. The male's "transcendence" of nature and society is made possible only through the subjection of the female to full-time maintenance of the social and physical connections that are, after all, indispensable for human existence. (Fee 1983; C. Keller 1986)

Catherine Keller, in her book *From a Broken Web* (1986), presents such an analysis of cultural association. In brief, she argues that in Western culture individuality has been stressed for men, to the point where it

---

[4] I say "naive observer," since Gilligan presented her results about differential tendencies to adopt one viewpoint or another as empirically observed tendencies, with overlapping statistical distributions (Gilligan 1987a: 25), rather than as biologically determined, disjoint viewpoints. More importantly, Gilligan viewed neither a purely masculine, nor a purely feminine, approach to identity or moral reasoning as adequate in itself. In Gilligan's view, while men and women tend to take different paths in moral development, probably due to differences in early childhood experiences, moral maturity for both sexes involves a complementarity between both types of moral reasoning: a "dialog between fairness and care" (1982: 174).
[5] The recent concentration on "hearing women's voices" may be necessary for the study of "connected" ways of knowing, since men currently have relatively little practice in self-definition through connection, while women are still socially rewarded fot it. The use of women subjects can also be a deliberate part of the design in a compensatory sense, because volumes have been written on "human" psychology using only male subjects.

takes on the perverse and extreme form of a mythical ability to live
without relatedness or interdependence with others. She calls this the
creation of the "separative" self. On the other hand, relatedness is
stressed for women, to the point where women are rewarded for trying
to let our own identities dissolve in marriage and family. This she calls
the "soluble" self. Pictured in a gender–value compass, we have

M+	F+
individual	related
M-	F-
separative	soluble

The positive complementarity represents a conception of humans as
differentiated individuals who are also interdependent and connected.
"Soluble" is the lack of "individual" and the perversion of "related."
"Separative" is the lack of "related" and the perversion of "individual."
The negative complementarity is the functional complementary of sexist
social and psychological roles, where individuality and relation are taken
on as distinct sex roles instead of incorporated into each person. The
positive complementarity is a self-identity that includes both elements of
individual distinction and of connection to others. The negative elements
refer to the extremes of femininity or masculinity, when the complementary cross-gender element is lacking. People who are overly connected
have too little idea of themselves as distinct persons; they may define
themselves only as others see them, or care for others to the extreme of
failing to see themselves as also worthy of care and respect. This seems
to be a vice that particularly affects women in Western middle-class
culture, who are encouraged to sacrifice themselves for their husbands
and children. On the other hand, people – and in contemporary culture
it is disproportionately men who have the expectation and the opportunity – who pursue individuation to the point of cutting themselves off
from relationships, end up isolated and uncaring. The feelings of vulnerability and loneliness that accompany isolation may breed attempts to
recreate the only kind of connection consistent with extreme self-individua-
tion: relationships based on control and domination, rather than on
empathy and mutual concern. Only in recognizing that both individuation and relation are important in defining human identity, is the
foundation laid for mature self-identity and responsible, non oppressive

human relationships. This analysis of separation and connection will form the basis for much of the analysis in later chapters of this book.[6]

The separation/connection dualism also has important ties to cultural interpretations of the relation between reason and emotion – reason, of course, being associated with masculinity and emotion with femininity. Philosopher Martha Nussbaum (1993) has outlined how in much of the Western philosophical tradition (and in some Eastern traditions as well) rational judgment has been associated with an ideal of self-containment and impermeability, that is, of the wise person as someone who is complete, invulnerable, and impervious to fortune because of their complete self-sufficiency. Emotions, in these traditions, are considered as opposed to rationality since to be affected by something not under the control of one's rational will is taken as a sign of weakness and vulnerability. Emotions are "holes, so to speak, in the walls of the self" (Nussbaum 1993: 11). She reinterprets emotions as playing an important part in truly rational judgment: in a world in which human life is in fact vulnerable – to mortality, illness, want of all kinds – emotional acknowledgement of need is, though sometimes painful, a prerequisite for good judgment. With notions of reason being highly associated with notions of objectivity and adequacy in current scientific (and economic) study, this reinterpretation of the role of emotion will also play an important role in the later analysis in this book.

SEXISM IN THE COMPASS

I have presented the diagram as if sexism does not exist, because I argue that the model is a useful tool for envisioning how we might think of gender in a nonsexist way. In the present-day situation, however, I have found (and expect to find more) problems of sexism popping up at every turn. It is simply much easier, in constructing these tables, to come up with the M + and F − content of any concept than to find words for negative masculinity and positive femininity. The legacy of sexism makes positive femininity, and the negative effects of the lack of positive femininity, almost invisible.

Consider, for example, how one would complete a gender–value diagram with the term "virility" (meaning "manly vigor") as its masculine–positive term. The lack of virility is "emasculation," which is

---

[6] Robin West (1988) proposes a strikingly similar diagrammatic analysis of the separation/connection issue, which was unknown to me at the time of my design of this compass. West, however, finds the source of gender distinctions in divergent material and existential "natures" of the sexes (though she moderates this somewhat in her concluding section). I locate the gender associations primarily at the level of cultural belief. Val Plumwood (1993) contains a recent treatment of the separation/connection issue. She calls isolation "hyperseparation," and solubility "merger."

a term in common use and which belongs in the feminine–negative quadrant. There exists a term, "muliebrity," whose definition is "womanliness" or the feminine "correlative of virility," but this is a very obscure word, to say the least. There exists no term suited for the masculine–negative quadrant:

M+	F+
virility	muliebrity
M-	F-
?	emasculation

The term that belongs in the lower left-hand cell should by analogy to "emasculation" be "effemination," but the word "effeminate" already exists and signifies an abundance of feminine (presumably negative) traits, not the lack of feminine positive traits. Even when one does come up with positive complementarities, one finds oneself dealing with expressions like "embodied rationality" or "social individuality" that sound awkward and vague in a society used to thinking in terms of dualisms and clear demarcations. Extend this problem to all areas of discourse, and it becomes obvious why much feminist scholarship is devoted to analysis of language, and why at times the process of communication is frustrating and slow.

Sexism is also historically wound up in previous attempts at a more complex understanding of gender. I can identify, with caution, the diagram that originally started me thinking along the lines of the four-quadrant diagram. I found something similar in Aletha C. Huston's 1983 work on sex-typing, which in turn drew on earlier studies by Sandra L. Bem (1974) and by Eleanor E. Maccoby and John C. Masters (1970). The central contribution of these studies was to envision masculinity and femininity as separate dimensions instead of as opposites in the same dimension. The problem with these studies is that the criterion for positive value was identified as "social desirability," a criterion that functions rather strangely in a sexist society. In a sexist society, maintenance of accustomed patterns of oppression and victimization receive social approval. Bem's original "positive" traits rated by students as especially desirable for women included "childlike," "gullible," and "yielding"; the masculine-identified "positive" traits included "aggressive," "dominant," and "forceful" (Bem 1974: 156). Such a conceptualization of gender was associated with the term "androgyny," which has

18

since lost respect in many feminist circles. I hesitate to apply that term to what I have outlined as the positive complementarity because of inappropriate associations it may call forth.[7] To the extent that "androgyny" is associated with Bem's earlier work and high ratings on both masculine- and feminine-identified "socially desirable" traits, it suggests that combining "yielding" and "dominant" is somehow possible, and a good thing. I would identify both of these as negative terms – perversions of "sensitive to others" and "assertive," respectively. In a gender-value compass,

Positive

asserts own interests	sensitive to others

Masculine _____|_____ Feminine

insensitive to others	yields to others

Negative

In this more complex understanding of gender, it is the balance of self- and other interests that is valued, not the sex-stereotyped extremes.[8] Unlike Bem's and Maccoby and Masters's work, my diagram is not (at least in its use here) empirically based. Rather, it is theoretical, subjective, and visionary. I suggest that it can be used to investigate what the gender and value associations of concepts might be in a world where sexism is absent.

Conceptual sexism can be characterized as an ability to see only the $M + /F -$ aspects of the full diagram, or as a tendency to reassert a hierarchy on top of it (e.g., "relatedness is good, but individuality is better"). The central task of the feminist project on gender, then, as I see it, is the exploration and valuation of the feminine–positive and the exposing of the masculine–negative. This intellectual project is associated both metaphorically and by the position of individual feminists in particular and varied relationships to other dimensions of difference – racial, class, cultural – that have been similarly distorted by unidimensional thinking. This intellectual project can also be turned towards the examination of sexist influences in particular areas – such as academic economics.

---

[7] For a study of the development of the concept of androgyny and critiques of the same, see J.G. Morawski (1987). See also further discussion in Chapter 10.
[8] The distinction between self-interest and selfishness is further discussed in Chapter 9.

2

GENDER AND ECONOMICS

THE ISSUE

Understanding gender as a cognitive construct, and having untied the knot linking gender associations to judgments of value, we can now examine the influence of gender on the discipline of economics. Economics has been heavily influenced by the confusion of masculinity *ipso facto* with high value, as evidenced in both contemporary definitions and in the history of economics as a science. This confusion has been to its detriment. The methodology, theories of behavior, definition, and objectivity of economics can be much improved by applying new thinking about the relation of gender and value.

THE DEFINITION OF ECONOMICS

The diversity of endeavors undertaken by economists suggests that there is no easy, definitive description of what economics is, and what projects are outside its realm. I will limit my comments to current mainstream North American economics (often referred to as "neoclassical," in a broad sense) as I am not myself familiar enough with other branches such as Marxism or modern institutionalism. Clearly the central concept in mainstream economics is that of "the market." On this even economists as diverse as Robert Heilbroner and Gary Becker agree. Heilbroner traces the historical beginning of the field of economics to the ascendance of the market system over systems of "custom or command" (1986: 20). Becker (1976) simply carries this conception to its logical extreme in seeing markets in all aspects of human behavior. The idealized market is a place where rational, autonomous, anonymous agents with stable preferences interact for the purposes of exchange. The agents make their choices in accordance with the maximization of some objective function subject to resource constraints, and the outcome of their market interactions is the determination of an efficient allocation of goods along with a set of equilibrium prices. The prototypical market is one in which

20

tangible goods or labor services are exchanged, with money facilitating the transactions, and in which the agents are individual persons. The prototypical scholarly work in economics is an article that studies market behavior using sophisticated mathematics to formalize the model in a "theory" section, accompanied by econometric analysis of data in an "empirical" section. Few works in economics follow the prototype exactly – the "agent" may be a household, firm, or even a country, for example, instead of an individual, or the empirical work may be left "for further research" or be ignored entirely – but for a work to be accepted as "being economics" it must bear a family resemblance to the core model. This definition of economics is wide enough to include research on dual labor markets, intra-firm behavior, satisficing, bargaining, cooperative aspects of markets, the role of government, aspects of finance, the distribution of wealth, human capital, fertility, and many other areas, but some areas are considered more central than others. The less a work has in common with the prototype the more it will be considered to be "on the fringe" or "not economics at all." Discussions of comparable worth (i.e., that jobs primarily held by women might be paid less, just because women generally do them), for example, violate the centrality of the idea that prices are set by market forces, and thus the subject is usually demoted to the realm of politics. Papers that consist of "just words" are rarely recognized as "economics" – you might see them in the American Economic Review as presidential addresses, or in clearly suspect journals such as those that deal with history or philosophy.

While the description of economics according to a prototype covers the wider range of what economists do, an alternative definition of economics in terms of a particular method alone has gained increasing influence. High status is given to the formal, mathematical model of rational individual choice (Nelson 1993b). Work which neglects to use such a model, no matter how "economic" it is in the other senses given above, is dismissed by those who hold this view as mere ad hocery. The common use of Varian (1984) as the core graduate textbook, and the direction taken in much of the recent debate on "microfoundations of macroeconomics," are evidence of the power of this view.[1]

Table 2.1 lists a number of contrasts that underlie current definitions of economics, and characterize the nature of economic research. In the

---

[1] The reader unfamiliar with contemporary mainstream economics might want to examine Varian (1984) to get an idea of the status currently given to the mathematical model of individual choice. This book, which requires that the student not only be comfortable with calculus and linear algebra but also with multivariate calculus and real analysis, and which declines to mention any "real world" institutions, is used in most Ph.D. programs in economics as the core text. I believe that such first-year graduate classes play a key role in the selection (and self-selection, since many intelligent students decide that this is not for them) of economists.

Table 2.1 The contemporary definition of economics

Core	Margin
Domain:	
public (market and government)	private (family)
individual agents	society, institutions
efficiency	equity
Methods:	
rigorous	intuitive
precise	vague
objective	subjective
scientific	non-scientific
detached	committed
mathematical	verbal
formal	informal
general	particular
Key assumptions:	
individual	social
self-interested	other-interested
autonomous	dependent
rational	emotional
acts by choice	acts by nature
Gender/sex associations:	
masculine	feminine
men	women

top section on the left are the items usually considered to define the core subject matter of economics: the public arena (meaning markets, and perhaps government), individual agents, and efficiency issues. This definition of the domain is not self-standing, however, but implicitly relies on suppression of the nonpublic, nonindividual, and extra efficiency terms on the right: the private realm (meaning the family), society and institutions, and fairness or equity. Similar dualisms underlie the image of economic methods as rigorous, precise, objective, and scientific. Objectivity is assumed to be assured by adherence to positive (i.e., value-free) analysis, an arm's-length detachment from practical or political concerns, the use of formal and mathematical methods, and the search for ever more general theories. This image is defined in opposition to notions of intuition, vagueness, subjectivity, political concern, verbal and informal analysis, and explanations of particular phenomena, all of which are assumed to be less than scientific. The subject of the economist's model world is an individual who is self-interested, autonomous, rational, and whose active choices are the focus of interest, as opposed to one who would be social, other-interested, dependent, emotional, and directed by an intrinsic nature. In many ways, this description resonates with the economist's self-image as well.[2] Clearly, the lefthand-side of this table does not describe all of economics. But it does describe tendencies so strong that any work which deviates from the standards becomes in some way marginalized. Specific examples of the way in which the dominant view blocks out alternative topics and modes of analysis will be developed at great length in Part II of this book.

The definition of economics is not immutable. Some working economists may, of course, see themselves as working in an age-old process of creating ever closer approximations to Truth. The idea that economics is socially constructed should not, however, be novel to anyone with an interest in methodology or the philosophy of science, or who has ever heard of the ideas of Thomas Kuhn (1962). As expressed by economists Bruce Caldwell and A. W. Coats (1984), "reality is everywhere dense. Observation thus requires selection. All description is from a point of view." Economics, as a human endeavor, reflects human limitations in understanding a reality that is always just beyond our grasp. Economics, as a social endeavor, reflects some points of view, favored by the group that makes the rules for the discipline, and neglects others.

THE GENDER OF ECONOMICS

While the intensity of resonance of gender associations with the columns of Table 2.1 – men and masculinity for the left and women and femininity for the right – will vary individual by individual, it is clear that the dominant cultural understanding in the modern United States associates men and masculinity with being public, active, and rational, and women and femininity with being private, passive, and emotional. The role of the conception of gender as a hierarchical dualism in the construction of economics can be elaborated on two different margins: in the way in which economics is defined as being embedded in a multitude of projects that together constitute "science," and in the way in which economics is differentiated from other scientific disciplines, especially the other social sciences.

The historical and contemporary links between thinking about science and thinking about gender have been explored in a plethora of recent works by feminist scholars, including *Reflections on Gender and Science* by Evelyn Fox Keller (1985) and *The Science Question in Feminism* by Sandra Harding (1986), as well as numerous articles and anthologies (Bleier 1986; J. Harding 1986; Harding and O'Barr 1987). Harding argues that:

---

[2] See, for example, Robert Frank *et al.* (1993), concerning economists' attitudes about self-interest.

Mind vs. nature and the body, reason vs. emotion and social commitment, subject vs. object and objectivity vs. subjectivity, the abstract and the general vs. the concrete and particular – in each case we are told that the former must dominate the latter lest human life be overwhelmed by irrational and alien forces, forces symbolized in science as the feminine. All these dichotomies play important roles in the intellectual structures of science, and all appear to be associated both historically and in contemporary psyches with distinctively masculine sexual and gender identity projects.

(Harding 1986: 25)

That is, science has been socially constructed to conform to a particular image of masculinity. A parallel idea of dualism, though with less emphasis on gender, can be found in Donald McCloskey's work on *The Rhetoric of Economics*. McCloskey asserts that "modernism" stresses the strict demarcation between scientific and humanistic, fact and value, truth and opinion, objective and subjective, hard and soft, rigorous and intuitive, precise and vague, male and female (1985: 42).

There is evidence of a self-conscious striving for masculinity in the early formation of the ideals of modern science. Evelyn Fox Keller's *Reflections on Gender and Science*, Carolyn Merchant's *The Death of Nature*, Susan Bordo's *The Flight to Objectivity*, and Brian Easlea's *Witch Hunting, Magic, and the New Philosophy*, investigate the gendered nature of the modern scientific worldview which arose during the sixteenth and seventeenth centuries. In this period, the predominant cultural conception of the relationship between humans and nature changed from one in which humans were seen as embedded in a female, living cosmos, to one in which men were seen as potentially detached, objective observers and controllers of nature, conceived of as mechanical and passive. The identification of science with masculinity, detachment, and domination of nature – and with superiority – and of femininity with subjectivity, submission, and connection to nature is explicit in some of the language used by the early scientists of this period to define their endeavor. Henry Oldenburg, an early Secretary of the Royal Society, stated that the intent of the Society was to "raise a masculine Philosophy . . . whereby the Mind of Man may be ennobled with the knowledge of Solid Truths." (Keller 1985: 52). The relation of masculine science to feminine nature is often expressed in terms of domination, as in Francis Bacon's words, "I am come in very truth leading to you Nature with all her children to bind her to your service and make her your slave" (Keller 1985: 39).

The definition of economics is embedded in the definition of modern science, but economics is also differentiated from science in general. As a social science, economics takes a "feminine" role *vis à vis* mathematics and the physical sciences. Human behavior would seem to most to be a "softer" subject than abstract math or the study of the physical world, less amenable to quantitative (as opposed to qualitative) description or formulation in terms of "laws." This presents a problem for those economists who, perhaps in order to maintain a clear-cut gender self-image, need to see their work as consistently masculine. Neoclassical economics is in fact based on the work of nineteenth-century scholars who denied any qualitative difference in subject matter between scientific economics and physics. Stanley Jevons, Leon Walras, Francis Edgeworth, and Vilfredo Pareto were explicit about their emulation of the physics of their time. To quote Francis Edgeworth,

> The application of mathematics to the world of the soul is countenanced by the hypothesis ... that Pleasure is the concomitant of Energy ... As the movements of each particle, constrained or loose, in a material cosmos are continually subordinated to one maximum sub-total of accumulated energy, so the movements of each soul whether selfishly isolated or linked sympathetically, may continually be realizing the maximum of pleasure.
>
> (1881, quoted in Mirowski 1988: 15)

While such "physics envy" may be less apparent in the present day, since physics has moved on from its nineteenth-century theories even if economics has not, the quantitative natural sciences are still looked up to by contemporary economists.[3]

Among social sciences, the masculine identity of economics is more secure. A favorite pastime of economists is dumping on, expressing bewilderment about, or ridiculing the lack of "rigor" in the other social sciences. Classifying a work as "sociology" is an especially quick and surefire way of silencing it by removing it from the territory of serious conversation of economists. The hierarchical relations between the social sciences are especially evident in the ranking of journals within academic culture: having an article accepted for publication in an economics journal seems to be considered a coup for a sociologist or political scientist, but a publication in a political science or sociology journal by an economist (or in a sociology journal by a political scientist) is no harbinger of professional advancement. It may even be seen as an embarrassment.

Why is economics perceived as more masculine? One reason may be that economics is blessed with a natural unit of measure – money – that

---

[3] The term "physics envy" has been used by Margaret Schabas (1993). For more evidence about physics wannabes, see Chapter 4. Note that my argument that single-minded physics envy is deleterious does not imply that borrowing wisely from this (or any other field) is harmful.

makes quantitative analysis easier. Another may be that economics as a profession has managed (whether by conscious intent, or more likely, by subtle gender structuring) to hold the line more strongly against the recent influx of women. Marianne Ferber (1990) notes that the fields of sociology, psychology, anthropology and political science all have a substantially higher percentage of women among new Ph.D.s than has economics. One would think that this might be tied in with the first reason, in that women in general tend to have less mathematical training than men. However, Ferber also points out that mathematics also has more women as a percentage of new Ph.D.s than does economics.

I suspect that other reasons going beyond the association of mathematics and masculinity can be found by looking at more subtle gendered aspects of the differentiation of economics from the other social sciences. The economist's conception of a person as an autonomous agent (consistent with the centrality of the market metaphor) is quite different from the sociologist's idea of persons as acting out social roles (consistent with a central metaphor of functional society). Economics deals with concepts of the individual, activity, choice, and competition which are identified in our culture with masculinity; the domain of sociology might be seen as involving the more feminine-identified concepts of the collective, passivity, determinism, and cooperative social relations. This is not to say that sociology is immune from the criticism that within its own structure it contains masculine biases, but only that *vis à vis* economics it takes the more "feminine" role. Economics also deals at length with issues of markets and government, realms traditionally considered masculine, while the subject matter of sociology more centrally includes the traditionally feminine realms of marriage and family. Such gender images may affect not only the way practicing economists perceive their subject, but also affect subtlety the self-selection of young students into the professions as they look for explanations that seem adequate to their own experiences and consistent with their own socialized gender-identity.

Have the properties associated with the "masculine" identity of economics served any useful purpose? I believe that they have, and do not want to leave the impression that I consider neoclassical economics to be evil incarnate. The emphasis on rigor can be seen as an attempt to avoid sloppiness, the use of mathematical formalism as a way of catching errors that might go unnoticed in ordinary language, and the emphasis on self-interest and competition as a way of avoiding a mushy sentimentality. So far, so good. But is sloppiness the only alternative to rigor? Empty rhetoric, the only alternative to precise mathematics? Is mushy sentimentality the only alternative to heartless competition? Within the usual dualistic metaphors for gender and economics, these are the only alternatives, and a "less masculine" economics could only be "emasculated." As long as masculinity is associated with superiority, the idea that economics could be improved by becoming less one-sidedly masculine makes little sense. But the discussion of gender and value in Chapter 1 was directed at undermining exactly this association of femininity with inferiority.

I propose here an analysis that retains both culturally shared gender constructs, and many common judgments about what is desirable in economics. In particular, I propose that we accept that terms like "hard," "logical," "scientific," and "precise," are masculine-identified and describe legitimate goals of economic practice. But I also propose that we think of gender and value as orthogonal dimensions as suggested in Chapter 1, and actively seek out what has been excluded from economics by the confusion of masculinity with value. This exercise is not definitive of gender in any sense, nor does it cover every possible term that could be used to describe economics. The idea of orthogonality is simply proposed as an alternative metaphor to the usual hierarchical dualism. As with any metaphor, it hides as well as exposes some aspects of the reality it is meant to describe.

GENDER, VALUE, AND ECONOMIC METHOD

The association of economics with formal, logical reasoning can be addressed in the framework of the gender–value compass. In the simple dualistic view, reason is conceived of as identical with formal logic and masculinity; any exposition not explicitly conforming to the laws of logic is identified as being illogical, and, by implication, inferior. Consider how economists' view of reason bears a resemblance to that of Thomas Hobbes, who wrote,

> When a man *Reasoneth*, hee does nothing else but conceive a summe totall, from *Addition* of parcels; or conceive a remainder, from *Substraction* of one summe from another . . . In summe, in what matter soever there is a place for *addition* and *substraction*, there also is place for *Reason*; and where these have no place, there *Reason* has nothing at all to do.
>
> (Hobbes 1651; emphasis and spelling in the original)[4]

Economics seminars, for example, are often built around a formal model and its formal implications, and bring in as an aside or heuristic device an explanation of the "intuition" behind the result. These "intuitive" explanations (quite in contrast to the alternative meaning of "intuition" in terms of a flash of inspiration) often include long and elaborate chains of verbal reasoning, carefully constructed analogies, and concrete examples. These explanations, however, are considered "softer" than the

---

[4] I thank David Sebberson for pointing out this reference to me.

formal models, and, like the proverbial "feminine intuition," unreliable and unrelated to true rationality.

A more sophisticated idea of what it means "to reason" and "to know," suggested in many works on metaphor and cognition (cited in Chapter 1), identifies reason instead with a complementarity of logic, on the one hand, and reasoning by other means, such as analogy or pattern recognition, on the other. For example, Howard Margolis (1987) expresses cognition as a combination of "reasoning why," or step-by-step critical analysis, with "seeing that," which involves a no less important perception of the bigger pattern. Georgescu-Roegen's (1971) distinction between "arithmomorphic" and "dialectical" concepts is helpful in suggesting terms for the missing feminine–positive, masculine–negative diagonal in the gender value compass. He calls "arithmomorphic" those concepts that can be manipulated by formal logic. Most of our thoughts, however (he argues), are concerned with forms, qualities and concepts that overlap with their opposites, and dealing with these requires "dialectical" thought. His examples of dialectical concepts include "good," "justice," "likelihood" and "want" (1971: 45). Another example of the contrast between logical and dialectical thinking is given by Margolis' discussion of the meanings of the word "or" (1987: 94). In formal logic, "or" means "either or both, and not neither." But in common usage its meanings are contradictory: in "Cream or sugar?" it means "either, both, or neither"; in a judicial decision of "$100 or 10 days" it means "either, but not neither and not both"; in a waiter's question of "soup or salad" it means "either or neither, but not both." Yet, in context, these are all meaningful and reasonable statements. It is hard to imagine any discussion of economic issues that would not rely heavily on such understanding of context.

The "position that dialectical concepts should be barred from science because they would infest it with muddled thinking," Georgescu-Roegen labels "arithmomania" (1971: 52). Logical reasoning can deal only with the abstract; attentiveness to context and substance requires dialectical reasoning. Such a richer understanding of the nature of rationality can be summarized in a gender–value diagram as

M+	F+
logical reasoning	"dialectical" reasoning
M-	F-
"arithmomania"	illogic

The extensive verbal explanations economists often call "intuition" are examples of dialectical reasoning, not merely cases of degraded or diluted logic. The identification of reasoning with logical reasoning alone ends up, in Georgescu-Roegen's words, "giving us mental cramps" (1971: 80). The usefulness of two-dimensional over one-dimensional thinking about gender and value comes from the exposition of relationships that are hidden by the usual pairing of reason–masculine–superior with intuitive–feminine–inferior. That simple dualism can be seen to involve the too easy collapsing of reason into logic and the false identification of other valid forms of reasoning with illogic.

Similarly, the idea that there are different kinds of knowledge can be pictured as

	scientific	humanistic
	inhuman	unscientific

where I use the term "scientific" in the sense of instrumental, technological ("how to") knowledge, systematically gathered from observation of phenomena "external" to the researchers' own consciousness, and "humanistic" in the sense of affective, introspective knowledge focusing on the "why" and "for what purpose" questions of human existence. Humanistic knowledge without at least a touch of the practical, outward-focusing approach I have labeled "scientific" is at best sterile (because it can have no effect on what actually happens), and at worst the ravings of a lunatic (if unique to a single person). But the elevation of scientific knowledge (implicit in the project of "demarcation" of science) without attention to human values could very well lead to the very efficient destruction of life on earth.

The emphasis on mathematics as the key to "rigorous" understanding in economics, and the downplaying of language as having any importance to the business of knowledge seeking, can be understood using the diagram:

	precise	rich
	thin	vague

29

The left side highlights aspects of mathematical language and the right side aspects of common language. The advantage of use of mathematics is the precision it supplies, as opposed to the vagueness or ambiguity that may be associated with words in all their diverse meanings. On the other hand, pure mathematics is precisely content-free; the application of mathematics to problems of human behavior can come only through the explanation of mathematical formulae as metaphors for some real world phenomenon, and this drawing of analogies involves the use of words. In the process, meanings beyond that immediately present in the mathematical analogy will also be suggested. Mathematics can certainly be helpful in overcoming the failings of imprecise words, but, if concentration is put on maintaining the gender boundary rather than on recognizing the value boundary, the failure of thin, empty mathematics may sneak in unobserved. Empty math, or "rhetorical math" in the pejorative sense, is described by Philip J. Davis and Reuben Hersh (1987: 58) as math that neither brings forth any new mathematical idea nor "leads back to the phenomenon being modeled." "Precision" is a virtue in economics; this analysis suggests we also consider "richness" to be good, too, and furthermore that we recognize the pursuit of precision alone, without richness, as a vice.

GENDER, VALUE, AND "ECONOMIC MAN"

While the above analysis can aid in developing a new and broader understanding of rationality, knowledge, rigor, and numerous other concepts that come into play in the definition of economics, this section applies the expanded metaphor for gender and value to the concept of individual agency. The point at issue here is not whether or not the assumption of individual agency can lead to fruitful hypotheses: there is no doubt that the assumption of "economic man" has been fruitful, especially as contrasted to the alternative hypotheses that human behavior is completely socially determined, as assumed in my caricature of sociology, or that it is materially determined, as in some variants of Marxism or perhaps in sociobiology. The problem is that when we limit the choices to an autonomy/determinism dualism, we limit ourselves to playing with only half a deck.

The conception of human nature underlying neoclassical economics is of an individual human as radically separate from other humans and from nature; the emphasis is on separation, distance, demarcation, autonomy, independence of self. Economists have carried out more than one suggestion by Thomas Hobbes. In addition to his writings on the nature of reason, Hobbes also wrote, "Let us consider men . . . as if but even now sprung out of the earth, and suddenly, like mushrooms, come to full maturity, without all kind of engagement to each other" (cited in

Benhabib 1987). *Homo economicus* is the personification of individuality run wild. "Economic man," the "agent" of the prototypical economic model, springs up fully formed, with preferences fully developed, and is fully active and self-contained. He has no childhood or old age; no dependence on anyone; no responsibility for anyone but himself.[5] The environment has no effect on him, but rather is merely the passive material, presented as "constraints," over which his rationality has play. He interacts in society without being influenced by society: his mode of interaction is through an ideal market in which prices form the only, and only necessary, form of communication. *Homo economicus* is the central character in a romance of individuality without connection to nature or to society.

Yet humans do not simply spring out of the earth. Humans are born of women, nurtured and cared for as dependent children, socialized into family and community groups, and are perpetually dependent on nourishment and shelter to sustain their lives. These aspects of human life, whose neglect is often justified by the argument that they are unimportant or intellectually uninteresting or merely "natural," are, not just coincidentally, the areas of life thought of as "women's work." If we grant that connection – to one another, and to nature – is indispensable for human existence, then *homo economicus* appears in a new light. Far from being the rugged individualist whose status as a modeling tool is dictated by rationality and realism, he might well be the projection or dream of a boy who, scared of the powers which might fail to protect his fragile hold on life, denies to himself his own dependence.

The idea that this conception of selfhood as radically separate from our fellow humans could be misleading and indeed dangerous is not unique to feminist scholarship. The way in which it leads us to ignore the sociality of our thought and existence has been pointed out by McCloskey and other scholars who investigate the role of rhetoric (McCloskey 1985). The way it causes us to neglect the physical basis of our thought has been emphasized by Lakoff and Johnson, who stress the "bodily basis of meaning, imagination and reason" (Johnson 1987). Not all criticism of this solipsistic view of individuality is this recent: Alfred North Whitehead wrote about the dehumanizing and self-defeating aspects of the modernist view in 1925, while Martin Buber pointed to its distortions of relationship in 1958.

To the familiar dualistic contrasting of individual to social identity, and individual agency to social or material determinism, the scholarship

---

[5] I use the pronoun "he" intentionally: the gender biases underlying the concept of "economic man" would by no means be overcome by replacing or alternating with the pronoun "she," in an attempt at cheap gender neutrality. See Frank and Treichler (1989) for the difference between gender-neutral and nonsexist language.

31

on gender adds contrasts of connection and isolation, "influenced" action and radical autonomy. The various conceptions of human nature, particularly in regard to the relation of the self to other humans and to nature, can be encompassed in a slightly rephrased version of a compass presented in Chapter 1:

individuated	connected
isolated	engulfed

That is, the conventional idea of identity stresses the northwest–southeast diagonal: the lack of any individuality or differentiation implies the dissolving or engulfing of the individual into the larger whole of nature or society. The gender connotations are "masculine" for the positively valued individuality and "feminine" for the undifferentiated state. But differentiation can go too far, into radical separation or isolation. The message of one strain of current feminist scholarship reviewed in Chapter 1 (and to be elaborated on in Chapter 3) is that connection and relation do not necessarily imply the dissolving of individual identity. The positive complementarity of the upper two terms in the diagram refers to the recognition of selfhood as including both individuality and connectedness or relatedness. Or, in Alfred North Whitehead's words, we are "organisms" who require "an environment of friends" (1925: 206). The boundaries between oneself and others and oneself and nature are not strict, but neither does this imply that one is therefore swallowed up. The separation of the gender/value dimensions creates a way of seeing that individuality is not definitive of the human condition.

Similarly, for the question of the locus of decision-making, the separation of the dimensions suggests alternatives to individual agency and social or material determinism:

individually agenic	influenced
radically autonomous	determined

The radically autonomous decision-maker admits no influence from society or nature: as the sociopath whose psychological development lacks the interactive aspects shared by the rest of society, or the anorexia nervosa patient who claims that eating is a "lifestyle" habit that she can do without. Or Economic Man, whose behavior can be described purely in terms of individual preferences, without recourse to any description of social context, preference formation or physical need. The feminist approach to economics that I am suggesting is by no means only "more sociological" than current economics, if what is meant by that is a turn to analysis assuming that agency lies entirely outside the individual. Economist James Duesenberry once wrote, "Economics is all about how people make choices. Sociology is all about why they don't have any choices to make" (1960: 233). To put it in the terms used by Martin Buber in his famous philosophical piece on identity and relation, *I and Thou*, the economist imagines "the world ... embedded in the *I*, and that there is really no world at all," while the sociologist (or sociobiologist) creates an image of "the *I* ... embedded in the world, and there is really no *I* at all" (1958: 71–2). The view of selfhood informed by this analysis means rejecting both radical autonomy and social determinism as paradigmatic stand-alone models of agency.

As an example, consider two extreme explanations of the increasing labor force participation of women over the last few decades. A radical "economic man" formulation takes preferences as given, so that all of the weight of explanation is put on changes in relative prices (arising from, for example, technological and demographic changes). Any apparent change in preferences is explained as epiphenomal, that is, as an outgrowth of price changes rather than a cause of changes in behavior. On the other hand, a radically social explanation puts all of the emphasis on social and political movements (in this case, feminism) and resulting changes in beliefs and norms, and none on individual incentives or choices. As narrow prior beliefs about the "real causes" of the phenomenon are allowed to constrain the analysis in both cases, neither is an adequate model for social science research. What is needed is research which is open to "both/and," not just "either/or."

GENDER, VALUE, AND THE DEFINITION OF ECONOMICS

If we were to change the central character in our economic story from the radically autonomous, isolated agent, who is unneedful of social contact and uninfluenced by physical concerns, to the socially and materially situated human being, what effect would this have on the definition of economics? As pointed out above, the central concept of modern economics is that of the market, the locus of exchange activity.

One direction might be to promote the study of markets with an eye to their social and institutional character, instead of always starting from the view that they are more or less corrupted versions of idealized (perfectly competitive, perfect information) markets. Arjo Klamer's (1989) project on "interpretive" economics, for example, captures some of this approach. Another direction is suggested by the dimension of physical connection. Kenneth Boulding (1986) has remarked on the loss of an ecological understanding of economics, as concerned with the biosphere. He argues that part of what he sees as the "failure" of modern economics results from the loss of an earlier understanding of economic life as being about both "how society was organized by exchange" *and* about "how society was 'provisioned'."

An understanding of economics as centrally concerned with provisioning, or providing the necessaries of life, has implications quite different from the idea of economics as centrally concerned with exchange. In the exchange view, the primary distinguishing characteristic of a good is whether or not it can be exchanged on a market, not what human needs or wants it may satisfy or what role it may play in a more global, ecological system. The choice of goods depends only on abstract preferences. This radical conceptual separation of humans from their physical environment implies, among other things, sterility of economics about questions of human welfare. In the provisioning view, on the other hand, there are qualitative differences between different goods and services. Cooter and Rappoport (1984) explain how the pre-1930s material welfare school considered needs for survival and health to be more economic than desires for goods more at the luxury end of the spectrum. While the dividing line between "needs" and "wants" may be far from distinct (the concept of "need" being clearly in Georgescu-Roegen's "dialectical" category), the admittance of a category of "need" implies the recognition of an inescapable dependence of human bodies on their physical environment that is lacking in the modern view. The tie of the deprecation of need to the deprecation of the feminine has been expressed by Muriel Dimen (in another context) as "Wanting, associated with adulthood, active will, and masculinity, is better than need, linked to infancy, passive dependency, and femininity" (1989: 42).

The primacy within market-oriented economics of the focus on "want," to the neglect of any consideration of the provisioning-related concept of "need," suggests the following gender-value diagram:

ability to choose actively	ability to discern what is needed
unlimited wants	neediness

The masculine quadrants suggest interpretation of the world as a world

34

of scarcity, hostile to human purposes, or the standard Lionel Robbins definition of economics as study of human choices in context of unlimited wants and scarce resources (1935). The feminine–positive quadrant, missing from economic analysis, is the sensitivity about oneself and one's relation to the environment that allows one to determine what is *useful*, not merely what gives the highest rating on some immediate pleasure/pain calculus. Anyone who has been a parent should recognize the skill involved in this activity in discerning the needs of one's children: all I suggest is that we also focus such "maternal thinking" (the term is Ruddick's, 1989) on ourselves. Note also that while resources are by definition scarce in relation to wants conceived of as unlimited, resources might (still) be abundant in relation to human needs.

The closest work in economics I have seen to this conception of how humans are actually involved in their natural environment is Amartya Sen's notion of "capability," which is "a feature of a person in relation to goods" (1984: 316). An individual's advantage, according to the capabilities approach, is not judged by his or her subjective, individual happiness, nor by the set of external resources at his or her command, but by what those resources would allow the person to be or to do. Sen further elaborates this approach, distinguishing among "functionings," like being adequately nourished, which may require various resources because of diversity between individuals; the range of functionings from which a person may choose, that constitutes his or her "capabilities set"; and "agency freedom," or the freedom to pursue one's own goals (which may include but are not limited to one's own functionings or well-being). Advantage, then, is judged according to a *relationship* between the individual and his or her environment, that recognizes the agency and individuality of the person while at the same time recognizing his or her constitution in physical and social relationships.

Without such an understanding of material connection, we have the scandal of professional economists working out endless theoretical yarns about preferences while a majority of people in the world live in a state of neediness apparent to any observer who has not lost her or his humanity. With an understanding that incorporates both choice and material connection, comes the possibility of abundance and a hospitable nature, if we choose wisely.

In highlighting the connections as well as the distinctions between humans, and between humans and nature, does a wider, encompassing view of economics then imply that economics has to be about "life, the universe, and everything?" (Adams 1983). I do not think so. The relationship of economics with other social sciences could be closer and more cooperative, of course, and based on shared understanding of the multiple dimensions of human experience (rather than imperialistic, based on imposition of the model of radical separativeness). But economics

35

need not be undifferentiated. As a practical matter, I suggest that our discipline take as its organizational center the down-to-earth subject matter of how humans try to meet their needs for goods and services. Economics should be about how we arrange provision of our sustenance. This core corresponds better to the common sense use of the term "economics" (and to the etymological roots of the term in the Greek words meaning "household management") than does the present central concept of the idealized market. This core grounds the discipline both socially and materially. Economic provisioning and the sustenance of life becomes the center of study, whether it be through market, household, or government action, or whether it be by symmetric exchange, coercion, or gift. This definition dethrones choice, scarcity, and rationality as central concepts, and relegates them to the status of potentially useful tools. It brings previously taboo or fringe subjects like power and poverty into the core.

FEMINIST, FEMININE, FEMALE: CONTRASTS

The direction I suggest for economics is "feminist" in that it revalues some of the concepts metaphorically associated with femaleness, and so leads away from masculine bias. It is, however, distinct from what some might call a "feminine" approach to economics, in which one simply emphasizes those stereotypically feminine characteristics that have been neglected in the current construction of science. Such an approach runs the risks of reifying masculine–feminine categories, glorifying feminine–negative aspects, neglecting the task of distinguishing the positive and negative aspects of masculinity, and, just like the current masculine construction of economics, viewing economic phenomena in a one-sided way when an encompassing vision would be more appropriate. For example, it might be considered more "feminine" to model a particular phenomenon in terms of its aspects of cooperation rather than in terms of its aspects of competition or conflict, or to focus on social constraints instead of on individual agency. I would argue, however, that while aspects of cooperation have in general been unjustly neglected, substantial feminist insights into, for example, the understanding of the economics of the household have been accomplished by denying the existence of total cooperation within the household and instead noting the actual presence of conflict, and by rejecting common dictatorship models of the household (mislabeled as "altruistic" in a particularly glaring example of blindness to issues of power) in favor of attributing some form of agency to female actors (Folbre and Hartmann 1988). A feminist approach, while revaluing the positive aspects of femininity, does not then limit one to using those categories of analysis that happen to be in the socially created cognitive category of "feminine."

The feminist rethinking I advocate is also not the same as "female" economics, considered suitable for women economists or brought about purely by the inclusion of women in the profession. The argument made about the source of gender bias in economics is very important here; there is some subtlety to my argument that is often missed. While it is obvious that women have largely been excluded from the creation of modern knowledge, and that science is hence predominantly "masculine" in a purely social or demographic sense, my argument does not take this as the primary causal factor. Instead I argue, as do such theorists as Evelyn Fox Keller (1985, 1987, 1988), that it is *not* the case that because women have been excluded, science has not been able to benefit from "feminine" insights. This would imply that women somehow "by nature" think differently from men, and would "bring something different" to economics, as we are allowed into the club. The direction of causality in the line of feminist thought I present is the reverse: because science has grown up in a society in which everything thought to have the feminine gender, that is, which is cognitively associated with femininity and women, has been devalued, therefore women have been excluded from science. This takes the emphasis away from differences between men and women, and puts it on the common achievements that might be made by both men and women if sexism, (i.e., the systematic devaluation of women and things associated with women), were to be overcome. Certainly men and women have, on average, had very different experiences in a society structured by sexist expectations; but the importance of differences in experiences should be linked to the social structures and not simply biology. Certainly more women should be encouraged to enter economics; but, since women undergo a strong socialization process in entering the profession, entry in and of itself is no guarantee that the one-sided masculinity of economics would change. Certainly men can help create a new, less gender-biased economics. However, if they find that they are working mostly with other men then perhaps they are not being as unbiased as they believe.

APPLYING THE ANALYSIS

Progress in this direction may be slow, in part because such progress requires a new vocabulary. The hierarchical dualism that links femininity with all things inferior is so ingrained in our cognition and our language that a feminist writer is often at a literal loss for words to express what she (or he) means. It is much easier to fill in the masculine–positive and feminine–negative quadrants in the gender-value diagram than to think of adequate expressions for the strengths associated with femininity and the dangers of unbalanced masculinity. One example of this problem was given above, where recourse had to be made to special terms coined by Georgescu-Roegen in discussing the question of rationality; another in Chapter 1, with the terms "virility" and "emasculation."

Economics could be improved by an exploration of feminine–positive ways of knowing and being, and the excising of masculine–negative perversions of the choice of subject and scholarly method. The positive–negative dualism should be the salient schema for judging the adequacy of economic research, rather than the feminine–masculine schema. An approach based on a new understanding of gender and value would incorporate all aspects of knowledge that are helpful in approaching a problem, whatever they may be, and would extend the possible subject matter beyond simply those areas that can be "squeezed and moulded" (the words are Francis Bacon's, in Weinreich-Haste 1986) into the form of a mathematically tractable model of an idealized market. After a brief excursion into the more philosophical issue of how we define objectivity, Part II of this book lays out several specific examples of how sexist bias in subject, model, and method have distorted economic analysis, and how a broader analysis can lead to richer knowledge and more adequate policy.

3

WHAT ABOUT OBJECTIVITY?

INTRODUCTION

"The proposed expansions of method, model, and definition proposed in the last chapter endanger economists' claim to objectivity," a reader might argue. "The further we diverge from current practice, the more we leave ourselves open to subjective influences," the reader might reason.

Feminists argue that scientific practice is already full of subjective and contaminating influences – they just happen to be of an "androcentric" (male-centered) variety and hence invisible to the majority of practitioners. Within the particular community of (male) researchers such aspirations seem merely natural or self-evident. (Culture, one wag has noted, is what everyone believes that *someone else* lives in.) In fact the notion that objectivity is attainable by isolated researchers through strict adherence to prescribed methods, emotional detachment, and separation from the object of study itself appears, on feminist analysis, to be an emotionally loaded, culturally created construct. Rather than jump to the other side of an objectivity/subjectivity dualism, however, many feminist theorists have sought to redefine objectivity in line with a notion of science as socially constructed, and scientists as social beings (e.g., Alcoff and Potter; Antony and Witt, 1993).

This chapter looks at the various ways in which the high value given to unbalanced masculinity has influenced ideals of science, and investigates a new view of objectivity. The first chapter in Part II will apply the concepts set out in this chapter for science in general to economics in particular, within an historical context.

DETACHMENT IN SCIENCE

As noted in Chapter 2, Susan Bordo (1986, 1987), Evelyn Fox Keller (1985), Carolyn Merchant (1980) and others consider acceptance of the Cartesian model of objectivity, based on dispassion and detachment, to

39

be an outgrowth of anxiety created by the loss of the medieval feeling of connection to nature. If science has been considered masculine, one may wonder where the feminine fits into the picture. Karl Stern's book on philosophy beginning with Descartes is entitled *The Flight from Woman* (1965); James Hillman, in *The Myth of Analysis* (1972) writes, "The specific consciousness we call scientific, Western and modern is the long sharpened tool of the masculine mind that has discarded parts of its own substance, calling it 'Eve,' 'female' and 'inferior'" (quoted in Bordo 1986: 439–41). The counterpoint to rational, detached "man" is:

> woman [who] provides his connection with nature; she is the mediating force between man and nature, a reminder of his child-hood, a reminder of the body, and a reminder of sexuality, passion, and human connectedness. She is the repository of emotional life and of all the nonrational elements of human experience.
>
> (Fee 1983, 12)

In the Cartesian view, the abstract, general, separated, detached, emotion-less, "masculine" approach taken to represent scientific thinking, is radically removed from, and clearly seen as superior to, the concrete, particular, connected, embodied, passionate, "feminine" reality of mate-rial life.

If the perception of oneself as separate or detached from the world is a particularly masculine style of self-identity, what implications can be drawn regarding traditional ideals of "scientific detachment"? A tradi-tional view of gender and value, which tends to associate masculinity with positive value and femininity with inferiority, would simply confirm masculine detachment as an unequivocal virtue. A view that overcomes this too simple dualism recognizes that an area that has been developed largely by men in an atmosphere of gender duality may tend to reflect distinctive masculine hopes and fears.

Of course, one need not totally fear or disparage femininity in order to find the masculinity of science reassuring, rather than disturbing. Feminine values of connection may be encouraged in realms in which they are perceived as proper, and from which they do not venture out to interfere with "hard" science. Women, it might be noted, are encouraged to be the emotionally supportive wives of the scientists. Intellectuals of either sex, it may be argued, are allowed to draw inspiration from feelings of unity with nature – as long as the application is to poetry, not science. The idea of "separate spheres," however, polarizes masculinity and femininity, science and the humanities, and rules out the kind of complementarity discussed above. By eliminating femininity in science, is science made strong in its radical detachment? Or, instead, by going to such extremes to avoid over-attachment, is it left weakened and distorted by insufficient attention to connection?

These questions can be addressed by examining the various ways in which ideals of detachment enter into the idea of science, and considering, at each stage, the suggestions of feminist and allied scholars on the possibilities of alternatives to the ideal of radical detachment. Consider detachment as operating in the current definition of objectivity on several fronts: detachment from social influences, detachment from the subject of study, detachment from fellow researchers, detachment from practical or immediate concerns, and detachment from partisan ties.

Detached from social influences

One myth surrounding modern science is that science, or at least "good science," is beyond the reach of social influences. The evaluation of scientific programs can be based on the mandates of its methodological principles, which comprise, in Imre Lakatos' terms, its "internal history." If sometimes the social, political, racial, gender, or economic environment of the creation of scientific work influences the content of scientific theories themselves, it is assumed only to be in the direction of irrationality. These deviations can be classified as "bad science." The "external history" of the scientific endeavor serves to explain the non-rational aspects of scientific developments, but is not central to the evaluation of scientific programs (Lakatos 1971: 9).

Challenges to such a detached image of science, as existing above and beyond the actual living environments of its human creators, has recently come under fire from many scholars. The "strong program in the sociology of knowledge" associated with the work of David Bloor (1991) takes as a main tenet that successful, rational scientific programs are just as amenable to sociological explanation as the unsuccessful, "bad science" ones.[1] From a feminist perspective, Elizabeth Potter (1988: 141) points out that feminists have uncovered numerous instances in which "even scientific theories that are 'good' by all the standard criteria – e.g. they are simple, elegant, fruitful, internally consistent, externally coherent with the received paradigm, predictive and so on – are androcentric or sexist". She argues that such biases can enter scientific theory through "coherence conditions" such as assumptions about the goodness of particular analogies, and gives an example of political and gender-related motivations for seventeenth-century assertions of the passivity of matter. Karin Knorr-Cetina (1991: 107) has argued that "'culture' is inside the *epistemic*, and the . . . study of knowledge, must also concern itself with *the cultural structure of scientific methodology*" (emphasis in original). Her examples illustrate that there is not one, but rather several, "scientific

---

[1] A previous review of the "strong program" and its possible relation to economics is in Coats (1984).

methods." Other scholars in what is loosely called the "social construc-tionist" school also "invite us to consider the social origins of taken-for-granted assumptions" (Gergen 1985: 267). Sandra Harding (1993a, b) and Donna Haraway (1991) argue for acknowledgment of the social and historical contingency of knowledge from starting points in feminist theory. When science is seen, not only as a pursuit of rational understand-ing, but, just as importantly, as an activity undertaken by human beings in particular cultural environments, the usual distinctions between "good" and "bad" science, or "internal" and "external" histories, become obstacles rather than aids to clear thinking.

Acknowledgment of the socially influenced nature of knowledge does not, however, leave only radical relativism as an alternative. Philosopher Sandra Harding (1993a, b) calls the usual, detachment-based notion of objectivity "weak objectivity," because it excuses the social community of science from the domain of criticism. The quest for reliable knowledge is enhanced, not damaged, by reflection on and critical examination of previously ignored cultural influences. The alternative advocated is not relativism or subjectivism, but a strong form of objectivity (Harding 1993a, b), which takes the location of the knower into account. Philoso-pher and economist Amartya Sen (1992) uses the term "positional objectivity" to describe "an objective inquiry in which the observational position is specified (rather than being treated as an unspecified intrusion – a scientific nuisance)." He argues that any attempt at position-independent objectivity must build on positional views (i.e., be "trans-positional"), rather than ignore the position-dependence of views.

Detached from the subject of study

The approved position of the scientist relative to the object or phenom-enon to be investigated is often described as one of detachment or distance. An investigator who is involved in, influences, is influenced by, or has an emotional connection to the object of study is often considered to have insufficient objectivity.

Evelyn Fox Keller argues that such a conception of objectivity, which she refers to as "objectivism," itself has an emotional foundation: "The scientist is not the purely dispassionate observer he idealizes, but a sentient being for whom the very ambition for objectivity carries with it a wealth of subjective meanings" (1985: 96). Objectivism does not describe the position of the scientist in actuality, but is rather an emotionally potent romance rooted in masculine anxiety about connec-tion. Complete detachment is impossible. This should be obvious in the social sciences, where the researcher may be a member of the society that he or she wishes to examine. It is also a fact in the physical sciences: the recognition of how the interference of the researcher affects the subject of study yielded the Heisenberg uncertainty principle in physics. The pretense of detachment sustained by objectivism only hides such phenomena.

The rejection of objectivism, based on severance of subject from object, does not imply a rejection of the goal of reliable knowledge, a reversion to sloppy sentimentality, or a position of radical relativism. Keller's alternative notion of objectivity, which she calls "dynamic objectivity," is one that "actively draws on the communality between mind and nature as a resource" in the "pursuit of a maximally authentic, and hence maximally reliable, understanding of the world around one-self" (1985: 116). Mind and nature are neither disjoint, as in the separation/isolation model, nor fused, as in the connection/engulfment model, but "survive . . . in structural integrity" (ibid.: 165).

While examples of uses of "dynamic objectivity" can be found in the descriptions of work of other scientists (Easlea 1986), Keller's (1983) biography of Nobel Prize winner Barbara McClintock has become a touchstone for discussion. Entitled *A Feeling for the Organism*, the book describes McClintock's groundbreaking work on genetic transposition. In contrast to the more often heard descriptions of investigations in terms of detachment and conquest, McClintock's own description of her work uses "a vocabulary of affection, of kinship, of empathy" (1985: 164). In one passage, for example, McClintock describes how

> I found that the more I worked with them, the bigger and bigger [the chromosomes] got, and when I was really working with them I wasn't outside, I was down there. I was part of the system . . . It surprised me because I actually felt as if I was right down there and these were my friends. . . As you look at these things, they become part of you. And you forget yourself.
>
> (Keller 1985: 165)

Far from being part of a poetic or mystical flight *from* scientific knowledge, the attitude expressed by McClintock is, Keller argues, a crucial component in her coming to understand the complexities of her scientific field.

Detached from fellow researchers

Can scientific knowledge be gained by a researcher working alone? Will following a particular set of methods (which purport to guarantee objectivity, in the "objectivist" sense described above) be sufficient to assure the "scientific" status of an individual researcher's results?

"Scientific knowledge, like language, is intrinsically the common property of a group or else nothing at all," wrote Thomas Kuhn (1970:

210). The "social constructionist" view introduced above asserts not only the influence of culture on science, but also the social nature of scientific knowledge itself. "In this view the locus of scientific rationality lies not within the minds of independent persons but within the social aggregate. That which is rational is the result of 'negotiated intelligibility,'" writes Kenneth J. Gergen (1985: 272), in a review of social constructionism. However, Gergen argues, while constructionism rejects the idea that there is some way to gain direct access to transcendental, in-the-mind-of-God Truth, it

> does not mean that "anything goes." Because of the inherent dependency of knowledge systems on communities of shared intelligibility, scientific activity will always be governed in large measure by normative rules. However, constructionism does invite the practitioners to view these rules as historically and culturally situated.
>
> (Gergen 1985: 273)

Or, as put by feminist philosopher Helen Longino,

> The *objectivity* of individuals ... consists in their participation in the collective give-and-take of critical discussion and not in some special relation (of detachment, hardheadedness) they may bear to their observations. Thus understood, objectivity is dependent upon the depth and scope of the transformative interrogation that occurs in any given scientific community. This communitywide process ensures (or can ensure) that the hypotheses ultimately accepted as supported by some set of data do not reflect a single individual's idiosyncratic assumptions about the natural world. To say that a theory or hypothesis was accepted on the basis of objective methods does not entitle us to say it is true but rather that it reflects the critically achieved consensus of the scientific community. In the absence of some form of privileged access to transempirical (unobservable) phenomena it's not clear we should hope for anything better.
>
> (Longino 1990: 79; emphasis added)

This does not imply that it is acceptable for any group of people to choose to believe any desired theory – there is a real world, and a scientific approach requires that we seek evidence from that world to support or disprove our hypotheses. However, decisions about which hypotheses deserve investigation, and what constitutes acceptable and convincing evidence, are made by scientific communities. The process of understanding is "the result of an active, cooperative enterprise of persons in relationship." (Gergen 1985: 267). Isolated scientists are as mythological as isolated agents. Rigid methods only give a veneer of

44

objectivity (i.e., weak objectivity or "objectivism") after the ground rules are set by interests of a restricted community.

Similar ideas can be found as well in the writings of Paul Feyerabend (1975), Richard Rorty (1979), Helen Longino (1990), and others. Among economists, a similar view has been put forward by Donald McCloskey (1993), who suggests that we use the term "conjective" to refer to "what we know together".[2]

Detached from practical or immediate concerns

Yet another elevation of detachment comes in the association of high value with 'pure' research, that is, research separated from practical application. Of course, a certain amount of distance from immediate demands for practical fruitfulness may be necessary in order to give a researcher room for systematic study: a scientist who is always expected to work on the pressing problem of the day may only be able to do the shallowest of research. However, the diagram of gender and value is a reminder that detachment can be overplayed. In this case, one may fill in the quadrants with:

Positive

| | |
| concerned with understanding | concerned with practical problems |

Separated ———————————|——————————— Connected

| concerned only with abstractions | concerned only with "quick-fixes" |

Negative

The problem with overconnection with practical problems is a "quick-fix" mentality, where the "soft heart" of good intentions is unaccompanied by the "hard head" of understanding. The problem with overdetachment is, simply, irrelevance.

At this point, the question of the purpose or *telos* of science becomes unavoidable. What makes science a valuable endeavor worthy of human activity? Certainly there are myriad practical problems for which good

---

[2] Such scholars are, however, not necessarily nonsexist. See, for example, Sandra Harding (1991: 43) on Paul Feyerabend. While McCloskey's work is within a wider feminist viewpoint, I believe he gives undue emphasis to the notion that "women think differently."

intentions and "quick fixes" are inadequate solutions. We hope that the systematic study of natural, economic, and social causes of problems including hunger, disease, infant mortality, war, sexism and racism, and economic depression, will help lead to their alleviation. On the other hand, scientific endeavor also has its own esthetic rewards. Understanding has value in itself, as researchers stand in wonder at the beauty of new discoveries in astronomy or the elegance of a mathematical proof. The power hungry, of course, can envision a third sort of purpose for science: the aggrandizement of the control wielded by a particular interest group or country. The cynical researcher, to whom questions of *telos* seem romantic, may see no purpose to his or her work other than the personal gain of a steady paycheck and social approval.

The positive quadrants of the diagram suggest that an adequate vision of the purpose of science would see understanding and practical problem-solving as co-equal and complementary goals. Yet, in numerous discussions of science, the drive to understanding is taken as sufficient justification on its own. The question of the direction of scientific research is taken as self-evident, or as given by the "dictates" of reason, or by science's own "internal" momentum. Note, for example, the nonhuman location of the impetus in this contemporary description of economic theory (by which the author means the mathematical theory of individual choice) by Gerard Debreu (1991: 4): "Mathematics . . . is a forbidding master. *It* ceaselessly asks for weaker assumptions, for stronger conclusions, for greater generality. In taking a mathematical form, economic theory *is driven to* submit to those demands" (emphasis added). The actual subject of study may be of less concern than the process of understanding; allowing one's research to be influenced by anything other than logical progression may be considered, in fact, a sign of undesirable impurity. The questions of application are left to the politician, businessperson, or bureaucrat. Some may argue that this detachment from practical concerns, combined with the use of methods that guarantee "objectivity," makes science "value-free." Such a "value-free" science is considered, then, to be above the realm of purely humanistic concerns. The only moral imperative it recognizes is that of correctly following the implications of logic.[3] However, from a larger perspective, it is clear that such a view of science is implicitly built on another very important ethical judgment: the valuation of detachment over all connection. The contradictory nature of this position is revealed in its attachment of great value to detachment; in its passion for dispassionate analysis.

Of course, if research resources were unlimited, there would be no

---

[3] The way in which mathematical logic is perceived as having "moral authority" is discussed in Bloor (1991), especially p. 85.

problem with indulging all approaches to science. Scholars could entertain themselves and each other with limitless investigation of any subject whatsoever, no matter how minutely narrow or wildly divorced from practical concern. However, especially among economists, the issues of actual funding and the concept of "opportunity cost" should not be foreign. The romance of the individual scientist alone with his or her pure research is rather undermined by the real world issues of how the Department of Defense, corporations and other funding bodies like the National Science Foundation choose to set their priorities and allocate their funds. In a world of limited resources, the ethical implications of a decision to devote brainpower and money to a refinement of a logical structure 'demanded' by rationality are not limited to assuring that corollary one does in fact follow from axiom five. Resources devoted to this problem are resources not devoted to another perhaps more pressing problem. As the single-minded pursuit of detachment leads to the extreme of irrelevance, the ideal of "value-free" degenerates into the reality of "valueless." Returning to Gilligan's analysis of moral reasoning (Chapter 1), a feminist asks of science not only the question, "Does it follow the rules?" but also, "Is it responsible?"

In contrast to the philosophical tradition that sees ethics in terms of universal principles, unrelated to emotion or human connection, feminists after Gilligan have sought to elaborate the philosophical basis of the ethic of care. To balance much of the individualist, contractarian tradition of Hobbes, Kant, and Rawls, some feminists have undertaken a reconstruction of a moral philosophy in which personal relationships, empathy, and actual behavior also play an important role. In some cases, this has included combining feminist theory with elements more closely related to the traditions of Aristotle (Baier 1987; Benhabib 1987; Nussbaum 1992) and Hume (Baier 1987). Revalorizing these aspects of human identity associated, in the usual scientific worldview, with femininity and inferiority, allows the question of the purpose or value of scientific study to be brought back into the realm of human (rather than purely logical) affairs. While rules have their place in morality, empathy – and empathetic connection with those on whom the practical problems mentioned above are burdensome loads – also cannot be neglected.

Detached from partisan ties

Science, in its ideal form, should not be made subservient to any preconceived or politically expedient solution, or to the interests of any particular group. Conclusions should not be drawn in advance of (or in spite of) the evidence; results should not be judged on the basis of whether or not they offend powerful interests. Reference to a few blatant examples of such overconnection with political, religious or social interest – such as the Lysenko affair in Soviet genetics, or the promotion by certain Christian fundamentalist groups of Creationism – may usually be thought sufficient to warn the observer of science away from this trap.

What had usually gone unexamined until the rise in feminist scholarship on science, however, is how scientific research has often tended to reinforce the partisan interests of men. While literature on this issue is now legion, historical reviews of the study of reproductive biology by Nancy Tuana (1989) and Emily Martin (1991), are particularly amusing. The determination always to portray the male as the norm and as the active agent are shown to lead to theories that can only be described as bizarre.

The viewpoint of social constructionism suggests that science has no privileged position above the particular biases of its community of practitioners. While it is in the spirit of systematic research to seek to be rid of idiosyncratic and interested assumptions, total detachment is impossible. Acknowledgment of limitation, rather than the repression of difference, a seeking to understand across differences, and an opening of the community to previously excluded members, are the best defenses against partisanship.

NEW OBJECTIVITY

Strong objectivity, or objectivity that does not degenerate into "objectivism," is based not on an illusion of detachment, but rather on a recognition of one's own various attachments and on the partiality this location lends to one's views. The antidote to subjectivism and personal whim comes not from purity in method, but from comparison and dialog among various views within an open community of scholars. As Martha Nussbaum has put it, 'When we get rid of the hope of a transcendent metaphysical grounding for our evaluative judgments . . . we are not left with the abyss. We have everything that we always had all along: the exchange of reasons and arguments by human beings within history" (1992: 213).

Part II

APPLICATIONS

4

VALUE-FREE OR VALUELESS?

The Pursuit of Detachment in the History of Economics

THE HISTORY OF ECONOMICS

The history of economic thought is sometimes written as a progressive, unidirectional process of refinement, removing from the discipline what is sloppy, partisan, or biased and leaving only those elements consistent with the ideal of a rigorous, detached, and value-free science. In light of the discussion of objectivity in Chapter 3, this chapter looks at some ways in which the pursuit of detachment has been manifested in the historical development of economics. The "Statements of Purpose" or "of Principles" adopted by scientific professional associations offer a way of seeing how the members themselves conceived of the purpose of their gathering in association, and perhaps even the purpose of their investigative activity itself. The fact that such value-laden statements (the purpose of which is to persuade prospective members or the public of the worthiness of the associations' activities) come from groups that may also espouse the ideal of a "value-free" science, leads to the possibility of irony.

Three statements of purpose of major societies of professional economists founded in the U.S.A. are examined as case studies of economists' views about scientific detachment: the Statement of Principles of the American Economic Association adopted in 1885, the revision of these in 1888, and the Scope of the Society statement of the Econometric Society, adopted in 1930. While a full intellectual and social history of the influence of gender ideology on economics is beyond the scope of this chapter, the last section suggests some directions for future research in the history of economic thought.

THE STATEMENT OF PRINCIPLES OF THE AMERICAN ECONOMIC ASSOCIATION

Current American Economic Association members, who may think of the organization as a bit stodgy, are often surprised upon reading the content of the platform adopted by the founding members of the AEA in 1885:

1. We regard the state as an agency whose positive assistance is one of the indispensable conditions of human progress.

2. We believe that political economy as a science is still in an early stage of its development. While we appreciate the work of former economists, we look, not so much to speculation as to the historical and statistical study of actual conditions of economic life for the satisfactory accomplishment of that development.

3. We hold that the conflict of labor and capital has brought into prominence a vast number of social problems, whose solution requires the united efforts, each in its own sphere, of the church, of the state, and of science.

4. In the study of the industrial and commercial policy of governments we take no partisan attitude. We believe in a progressive development of economic conditions, which must be met by a corresponding development of legislative policy.

(Ely 1936: 144)

As recounted by historians of this period (Coats 1960; Rader 1966; Furner 1975), this platform was largely the work of Richard T. Ely, and was expounded in reaction to the perceived *laissez-faire* partisanship of older economists who rejected interventionist policies in the name of "natural law." Detachment is at best a minor theme in this case: the purpose of economics is clearly seen as the promotion of "human progress," and even more specifically, progress accomplished via state or legislative action. The "no partisan attitude" phrase in the last statement perhaps refers only to forswearing blind advocacy of the positions of particular political parties or industrial interests (and more specifically, to the free trade vs. protectionism debate of the time).

This platform generated a certain amount of ill-will among both joiners and nonjoiners who thought it was too much of a "creed" (Coats 1960). However, the platform also generated enthusiasm for the fledgling association among like-minded economists. J.B. Clark wrote in 1887 that "It does a certain work by giving character to the association during its early years" (Coats 1960: 559).

The accounts given by later historians of the controversies surrounding Ely and the new association are also interesting for what they imply about ideals of detachment. On one hand, it is interesting that this period is most remembered as a fight about method (the English deductivists vs. the German Historical School, in which Ely was trained). Methodo-logical disputes, of course, seem much more "scientific" than disputes about purpose or values. Ely himself disputed this interpretation:

> What we young fellows were concerned about was life itself, and the controversy in regard to methodology was simply a surface indication of forces operating more deeply. We believed that economics had, in itself, the potency of life. In the vast field of research which lay before us ... we felt we had opportunities *for service* of many kinds ... Looking about us with open eyes we saw a real labor question, whereas some of the older school talked about a "so-called labor question." We saw a good deal of poverty on the one hand and a concentration of wealth on the other hand; and we did not feel that all was well with our country. ... We thought that by *getting down into this life* and studying it carefully, we would be able to do something toward *directing* the great forces shaping our life, and directing them in such a way as to bring improvement.
>
> (Ely 1938 [1977], 155–6; emphasis added)

Besides emphasizing the human "service" aspects of professional purpose, Ely's words suggest in other ways an unusual affinity to what has been identified here as a "connected" way of seeing the world. His phrase "getting down into this life" is reminiscent of McClintock's empathetic and experiential vocabulary quoted in the previous chapter. The use of the word "directing" suggests a far less forceful, and more cooperative relation to economic forces than the usual vocabulary of "control."

While some historians who comment on these incidents do investigate the issues of purpose as well as of method, there is little indication of any sense that Ely's position may have contained elements of a valid scientific worldview. Mary O. Furner expresses a mild dissatisfaction with the irrelevance towards pressing social issues that resulted from later rejection of Ely's approach, but (perhaps necessarily, given the range of her book) presents no alternative (1975: 324). A.W. Coats writes simply that the later rejection of Ely's position led to the association's "permanent establishment as a strictly scientific and scholarly body" (1960: 566).

THE MODIFICATION OF THE STATEMENT OF PRINCIPLES

In 1888 a modified Statement was adopted by the American Economic Association (Tobin 1985):

OBJECTS
1. The encouragement of economic research, *especially the historical and statistical study of the actual conditions of industrial life.*

2. The publication of economic monographs.

3. The encouragement of perfect freedom of *economic discussion*. The Association, *as such, will take no partisan attitude*, nor will it commit its members to any position on practical economic questions.

4. The establishment of a bureau of information designed to aid members in their economic studies.

(American Economic Association 1895; emphasis added)

While this statement drops the earlier creed regarding the role of the state (which, given possible changes in conditions, may perhaps be validly criticized as "overconnected"), and is clearly less engaged and more self-serving than the earlier statement, it is still far from being an endorsement of pure detachment. The study of "actual conditions" is emphasized (as opposed to logical systems). While the Association is to take "no partisan attitude," nothing is said about the Association's members. In fact, "freedom of economic discussion" seems to presuppose diversity of views among the members, as well as an acknowledgment of the benefits of social review of research. This idea that research could be connected to practical investigation, reliant on discussion, and yet still scientific, while foreign to other discussions (and to some of the AEA members at the time as well), is not unique to this platform. A short paper (with no official status) by J.M. Clark (son of John Bates Clark) that appeared in the *American Economic Review* in 1919 expressed a similar view unusually clearly:

> Economic theory should be actively relevant to the issues of its time and it should be based on a foundation of terms, conceptions, standards of measurement, and assumptions which is sufficiently realistic, comprehensive, and unbiased to furnish *a common meeting ground for argument* between advocates of all shades of conviction on practical issues. *This is not an idea of scholarly detachment, for that may lead to studies that are inconsequential or irrelevant to the issues of the day. It is an ideal of scientific impartiality, which is a very different thing.*

(Clark 1919: 280; emphasis added)

The hallmark of scientific impartiality, for J.M. Clark as for the feminist theorists discussed in the last chapter, is something quite different from radical detachment. It is the struggle to form an adequate language for the discussion of a diversity of views.

The treatment of the AEA platform written in 1888, which still is apparently in effect (Tobin 1985), by later economists is again suggestive of an avoidance of connection. While the full charter is no longer printed in the official record of the meetings of the AEA, the most recent summary of it printed in the *American Economic Review*, while repeating most of the statements word-for-word, curiously fails to include the statement, "especially the historical and statistical study of the actual conditions of industrial life" (American Economic Association 1991).

THE SCOPE OF THE ECONOMETRIC SOCIETY

The "Scope of the Society" adopted by the Econometric Society on its founding in 1930 in Cleveland, Ohio (Roos 1933), stands in sharp contrast to the early AEA platforms:

> Econometric Society is an international society for the advancement of economic theory in its relation to statistics and mathematics. The Society shall operate as a completely disinterested, scientific organization, without political, social, financial or nationalistic bias. Its main object shall be to promote studies that aim at the unification of the theoretical-quantitative and the empirical-quantitative approach to economic problems and that are penetrated by constructive and rigorous thinking similar to that which has come to dominate in the natural sciences. Any activity which promises ultimately to further such unification of theoretical and factual studies in economics shall be within the sphere of interest of the Society.

Here one finds a blatant bid for scientific status, where scientificity is identified with quantitative analysis and radical detachment. There is no hint here that even individual members might be thought of as having positions on practical issues, much less arguing about them. There is no indication that discussion among members is thought of as helpful: the goal of the society is not to create a community of scholars, but to "promote."

Looking more closely at the language used to describe the relation of economics to the natural sciences in this passage, it is not too far-fetched to discern a sexual subtext. The experience of sexual intercourse from the male point of view is often reflected in historical and contemporary language regarding science, with imagery of penetration, probing, and piercing of nature, and the "overpowering rush" of scientific advance. While at times the metaphors suggest a loving intercourse, or at least a willing seduction of nature, at other times the combination of imagery of domination and of heterosexual intercourse suggests rape (Keller 1985, chapter 2; Easlea 1986; Weinreich-Haste 1986). Seen in this light, the Econometric Society passage may translate as, "Hey, guys, we want to penetrate and dominate, too!"

The lead article in the first issue of the Society's journal, *Econometrica*, further elaborates the perceived merits of a detached and quantitative approach. Joseph Schumpeter used this platform to express an interesting vision of mutual harmony, attained not through conversation or cooperation, but purely through quantitative analysis:

> There is high remedial virtue in quantitative argument and exact proof. That part of our differences – no matter whether great or small – which is due to mutual misunderstanding, will vanish automatically as soon as we show each other, in detail and in practice, how our tools work and where they need to be improved. And metaphysical acerbity and sweeping verdicts will vanish with it.
>
> (Schumpeter 1933: 12)

He explains the distance from practical issues by explaining that "even practical results are but the by-products of disinterested work at the problem for the problem's sake." In fact, he suggests that "practical men" such as politicians and persons in business are also distrustful "of anything not amenable to exact proof" (1933: 12).[1]

Unlike the AEA platform which has become largely hidden from view, the Econometric Society statement appears on the inside back cover of every issue of *Econometrica*.

TOWARDS A HISTORY OF GENDER INFLUENCES IN ECONOMIC THOUGHT

Consideration of the role of gender ideology in the history of economic thought opens up new angles from which to review the old stories.[2] A

---

[1] The theme of disinterested quantitative analysis is less pronounced in the lead editorial in the first issue of *Econometrica*, by Ragnar Frisch. Frisch is more hopeful of "stimulating discussions" being generated by members with "a variety of ideas." Perhaps surprising to the contemporary reader of the journal, Frisch predicted that "a considerable portion of the material appearing in *Econometrica* will probably be entirely non-mathematical" (Frisch 1933: 3).

[2] The examination of how masculine ideology (such as the idealization of radical detachment) has shaped the ideal of science is but one form of feminist analysis. Londa Schiebinger (1987) has identified three other feminist approaches to the history and philosophy of women in science. One other approach is to look for the "lost women" in the history of economics. Schiebinger has reviewed this literature for science in general; in economics such work includes Dorothy Thomson's *Adam Smith's Daughters* (1973) and Claire H. Hammond's study of late nineteenth-century American women economists (1993). Another is to trace the history of structural barriers, such as exclusionary university admissions policies or unequal access to mentoring, that have discouraged women's advancement in the discipline, as in Margaret Rossiter's work on women in science (1982). The third alternative approach looks at how women have been defined – and misdefined – in the history of thought. Nancy Folbre's work on nineteenth-century views of household labor (1991), or Michèle Pujol's (1992) tracing of historical thought on the determinants of women's wages, are examples in this category.

few of them – not by any means mutually exclusive – are outlined below.

On the level of broad cultural patterning, one may want to ask how dominant social beliefs about gender and dominant beliefs about science, both of which may undergo subtle changes over time, may have been mutually influential in particular historical epochs. Why was the Econometric Society statement in 1933 so different from the vision of economic science propounded in 1885? Could the explanation have anything to do with changes in beliefs about masculinity and femininity? Barbara Laslett (1990) suggests that the growth of objectivism can be seen as a reaction of men to, first, the piety, sentimentalism and "femininity" of nineteenth-century culture; and second, the loss by the end of the nineteenth-century of opportunities for men to prove their manhood via physically demanding occupations.

On an institutional plane, it is interesting to note the strength of the original melding (an objectivist would say "confusion") of social science with social reform in the history of social sciences in the United States, and the slowness of the process of their separation (Furner 1975; Rothman 1985). Is it only a coincidence that those parts of social science that were excised from economics in the name of objectivity also became those areas in which women gained preeminence? As economics moved away from social work and social reform, Jane Addams led the settlement house movement and Mary Richmond came to prominence at the head of the Charity Organization Society (Rothman 1985). Is it only a coincidence that when economics moved away from sociology, the latter was considered by some to be made up of "leftovers: marriage, the family, poverty, crime, education, religion, and sex" (Furner 1975: 298) – including exactly those areas of women's traditional activity and realms of pressing social problems? The history of economics should look not only at what parts of human activity have remained within the current understanding of the discipline, but also at the how and why of the cutting away of parts at one time considered integral.

Sensitivity to gender also suggests new issues in the examination of the work and lives of individual researchers. While it is possible for someone to take a more "connective" view of science while remaining sexist on other issues, is there any tendency of reduced sexism in one sphere to carry over into the other? It is interesting to note that Ely, who wanted to "get down into life" both acknowledged and encouraged the entrance of women into economics (1892, 1936: 150). In contrast, Luther Bernard, a leader in the push towards objectivism in sociology in the inter-war years of the twentieth century, railed against the "modern woman" and kept detailed diaries of his sexual exploits (Bannister 1987: 122, 132). Edward T. Devine, a student of Simon Patten who later became a leader in social work (Sass 1988: 237) argued that analysis of women's household (as well as market) labor deserved a central place in economic analysis (Devine 1894). In contrast, William Fielding Ogburn, another leader of inter-war objectivism in sociology, approved of many feminist positions but with the qualification (consistent with a bifurcation of separation and connection) that women should live up to their role as "unselfish angels" (Bannister 1987: 165). Are these misleading juxtapositions, too dependent on selective readings? If valid, do they fit into a larger pattern? Only further research can answer these questions.

Delving deeper into the lives of individual researchers, how much evidence is there that early childhood experiences (à la Chodorow) may have affected a researcher's leaning towards either detachment or connectivity in his or her image of science? While historians may express some reservations about post-mortem psychoanalysis, in some cases it is hard not to conclude that such experiences have played a role. William Fielding Ogburn (who underwent pre-mortem psychoanalysis) made no bones about stating:

> My father, planter and merchant, died in 1890 when I was four. Then began my long struggle to resist a dear mother's beautiful but excessive love. To the successful outcome, I attribute my strong devotion to objective reality, [and] an antipathy to the distorting influence of emotion.
>
> (quoted in Laslett 1990: 423)

Robert Bannister (1987: 89) suggests that William Graham Sumner's "keen sense of the inner and outer life, and of the separation of . . . sentiment and fact" may also have been due to early childhood experiences, but presents less definitive evidence. While cautions about such interpretations in the light of limited evidence or poor preparation in psychology on the part of the historian are certainly in order, there is no reason why such psychological investigation should be dismissed *a priori*. No reason, of course, except for a possible bias on the part of the researcher against "contamination" of "objective facts" with personal, emotional, or sexual elements. The usual bifurcation of a historical figure's intellectual life and private life may severely hinder illuminating research, and say more about the biases of the historian than about the reasons for the figure's views on economics.

Lastly, the gendered content of the language used to describe economic research needs analysis. Attention was drawn above to the use of the terms "penetration" and "domination" in the Econometric Society statement, and Ely's use of "direct" rather than "control," as examples. Gender-sensitive literary analysis would be another way to approach the tracking of the influence of gender in the history of economics.

The purpose of a gender-sensitive analysis of economic history is not to prove that detachment is evil, or that immediate practical relevance should be the only concern, or that all notions of objectivity should be overthrown in favor of a touchy-feely mysticism – or, need it be reiterated, that all women do (or did, or should do) economics differently than men. An approach that looks for effects of gender only in sex differences in practice – that looks at whether past women economists "did it differently" than men economists – is not likely to be extremely fruitful, given that the process of entering the discipline involves both significant self-selection and heavy socialization to the discipline's norms. More interesting is the examination of the gendered nature of the norms themselves, and the investigation of what a less masculine-biased economics might look like for both female and male practitioners. A major insight of feminist theorizing on the associations of masculinity with detachment, and femininity with connection, is that neither a purely detached nor purely connected manner of being in the world is to be highly regarded. What is needed, in the science of economics as elsewhere, is a complementarity between sufficient distance and sufficient attachment, a dialog between rules and responsibilities.

5

TOWARDS A FEMINIST
THEORY OF THE FAMILY

WHY A FEMINIST THEORY OF THE FAMILY?

Why do economists need a feminist theory of the *family*? This question has two parts: "Why a theory of the *family*?" and "Why a *feminist* theory?" Economists need theories of families for understanding how production, consumption, and savings take place within families: what is produced and consumed, and how these decisions are made. We need frameworks for understanding how families participate in markets, demanding and supplying goods and labor. We need to know how human capital is formed and maintained within families. We need to know how a family's demands and production translate into welfare levels for its various members. Any model of the effect of price changes, or taxes or transfers on family behavior must, implicitly or explicitly, rely on a theory of how families function. Beyond the social scientists' need to understand, lies the policy-makers' need to make wise policies. Better knowledge about what is happening in the family could improve policies related to child poverty and child support, household-sector savings rates, welfare and job training, the tax treatment of dependents and family-related expenses, social security, elder care, healthcare, and inheritance taxation, to name a few areas.

Why a feminist theory? First, while there are nearly as many types of feminism as there are types of families, the foundation of feminism is the repudiation of the belief that women should be subordinate to men.[1] In this, feminism in the West goes against centuries of legal, religious, and cultural theories that have conceived of the family as a male family

---

[1] The term "family," as used in this chapter, could mean any group of people related by blood or legal or quasi-legal bonds such as marriage, family registration, or adoption. Though it would be more accurate to talk about theories of families, rather than of "the family," much economic theorizing has been focused on Western, nuclear, co-resident families of heterosexual couples and their children. The term "household" can be used, loosely, as synonymous with family, but especially as referring to the effects of co-residence rather than of kinship.

"head," plus his dependent wife and children. While feminists recognize that in some cases the notion of such a patriarchal family may be nearly descriptively accurate, we reject the notion that such a structure is definitive or that it has positive normative value. A feminist theory is one that will not so easily collapse the analysis of a family into simple consideration of its "head." Second, a feminist theory is necessary because feminist insights into economic methodology suggest that we can achieve more than the thin analysis of the current narrow models of family behavior, whether based on a "head" or some more complex imagery.

THE MASCULINE BIAS OF CURRENT APPROACHES

Current approaches to the economics of the family are limited both by a masculine viewpoint on the subject and by a masculine-biased reliance on methodological individualism and formalism.

Three examples of masculine viewpoint

The most notable example of masculine bias concerning families in contemporary economics is, of course, simply the general absence of any attention to families at all. Take, for example, this quote from an economics textbook: "The unit of analysis in economics is the individual ... [although] individuals group together to form collective organizations such as corporations, labor unions, and governments" (Gwartney et al. 1985).[2] Families seem somehow to have escaped notice. Analyses of consumption, savings, human capital formation and well-being that explicitly treat the unit of analysis as a family of many persons, rather than as a single agent, are the exception rather than the rule. Chapters 6 and 7 will explore specific examples of the consequences of such neglect.

The work of Gary Becker and the other "New Home Economists" has been the major exception to this neglect. Gary Becker's (1974, 1981) model of the family, where all members act to maximize the utility function of the family "altruist," however, has been raising feminists' blood pressure since the mid-1970s when it first appeared. Formally, the household maximizes $U_h = U[Z_h, U_1(Z_1), \ldots U_n(Z_n)]$ where U_h is the utility of the "head," Z_h is the vector representing the "head's" own consumption, and U_i $(i = 1, \ldots, n)$ are the utility functions of the "beneficiaries" defined over their own consumption.[3] Becker's model is, undoubtedly, an elegant way to bridge the gap between theories of unitary households and the actual presence of multiple persons in a household.

[2] I thank Marianne Ferber for this example.
[3] The model may, of course, be adapted to include leisure and household production.

It certainly helped to bring family issues into the purview of economics, when previously they had been dismissed as noneconomic. As an empirical point, some households may indeed be dominated by the preferences of the household "head." The problem, from a feminist point of view, is the blatant sugar-coating of the model. The vocabulary of the "head's" "altruism," and the "voluntary" compliance by the "beneficiaries," who are nonetheless "selfish," makes the "head" sound like a good guy, a benign master of an otherwise dog-eat-dog family. "The 'head' of a family is," wrote Becker, that member who "transfers general purchasing power to all other members because he cares about their welfare." Although Becker wrote that his definition of the "altruist" or "head" does not rely on "sex or age," the weight of law, religion and tradition makes such a statement rather disingenuous. Undoubtedly, most patriarchal husbands would find it appealing to be portrayed as altruists. Such a glowing picture, is, however, quite extraneous to the actual workings of the model. Closer inspection of what makes the model work reveals that it is not exceptional sympathy for his fellow members that is central to distinguishing the "altruist" from the other family members, but power. The "altruist" is a person who has the power to transfer general purchasing power among all members (in early versions, net transfers to the "altruist" are not explicitly ruled out), as he happens to care about their welfare.[4] If he doesn't care very much, they don't get very much. If another member, say the wife, would prefer that more resources go to a third person, say a child, this is irrelevant: her altruism does not count because of her lack of power.[5] Similar criticisms of Becker's "altruist" model for its neglect of the issue of power have been raised by Robert Pollak (1985), Elaine McCrate (1987), Nancy Folbre (1988), Paula England (1993), Diana Strassmann (1993a,b), and others.

A less widely familiar example of masculine perspective comes from the theory of demographic effects on household consumption behavior. The Barten (1964) model of demographic effects posits that children (if the parents are taken as the decision-maker) or the wife and children (if the husband is taken as the decision-maker) have price-like effects within the "family" utility function, taken to be that of the couple or husband. Formally, the parent (or adult male) maximizes their (his) utility function

---

[4] Tauchen *et al.* (1991) present an interesting twist on the Beckerian idea of a dominant decision-maker: in their model, his utility function depends on the amount of domestic violence he inflicts.

[5] While this is offered merely as a hypothetical example, one of the most interesting empirical regularities yet to be explained by economic analysis is the observation (across several countries) that income under the control of women is more likely to be spent on goods for children or general household use (as opposed to personal consumption) than income under the control of men (Blumberg 1988; Pahl 1989; Thomas 1990).

over their (his) own consumption, formulated as $U = U[Z_1/m_1, Z_2/m_2, \ldots, Z_J/m_J]$, where the $Z_j(j = 1 \ldots J)$ are household purchases of J goods, and the m_j are functions of household composition that dictate how much of each total purchase the decision-maker is constrained to share with the other family members. The corresponding expenditure function shows the "implicit price" effects: $c = c[U, p_1m_1, p_2m_2, \ldots, p_jm_j]$. The higher the m_j, the larger the proportion of the purchase that must be shared, and the higher the "implicit price."

Barten originally presented his model at a 1964 symposium without any justifying "intuition," but this was immediately supplied by a discussant of his paper:

> I was led to Barten's formulation of the utility function by direct observation a few years ago when I realized in a moment of truth that when I was out with my wife and three children and I wanted some lemonade it was in effect costing me four shillings a bottle instead of one shilling a bottle. (My wife doesn't drink lemonade.) At the same time I also had the more pleasing feeling that beer was still only costing me 1s. 6d. a pint. (My wife doesn't drink beer either.) So I not only realized that it was rational for me in these circumstances to switch my consumption in favour of beer and away from lemonade, but I was stimulated to write down the utility functions that Barten has based his work on.
>
> (Brown 1964: 294)

Such an intuition, that it is not the thirst of the wife (who, one notes, gets nothing to drink in either case) nor of the children that guides purchases, but rather the preferences of the "head" in combination with price-like effects, has received easy acceptance in the literature. Angus Deaton and John Muellbauer (1980) point out this model's "very important insight; . . . Having children makes ice cream, milk and soft drink relatively more expensive and makes whiskey or cigarettes relatively cheaper." Or, as put by W. M. Gorman (1976), "When you have a wife and a baby, a penny bun costs threepence." The rational agent will substitute away from these newly expensive goods, towards whiskey and beer. While the model is widely used, it is only "intuitively" appealing to those who, first, find "natural" the model of the decision-making husband who cares only about his own consumption.

The problem of methodological individualism

Not all current models of family behavior rely on the positing of a dominant household "head." The most common approach in neoclassical theorizing is simply to treat the household as if it were an individual itself, consigning all its internal workings to a "black box." Most discussions of consumer behavior, for example, slip easily from a theory section referring to "the individual" or "the agent," to empirical sections based on household-level data. While such models are less obviously sexist than the Becker or Barten models, are they free of masculinist bias?

Paul Samuelson, in 1956, suggested that decentralized spending of income, dictated by a family "consensus" or "social welfare function" defined over the vector of member utility functions, would be sufficient to justify the "as if" treatment of household behavior as individual behavior. Formally, the household maximizes a social welfare function defined over individual utilities, $U[U_1(Z_1), \ldots U_n(Z_n)]$. Because of the assumption that, once income has been allocated among the members they will proceed to spend on their own, Samuelson notes that his "family must be a family of adults, or at least of very unusual children."

More recently, attempts have been made to use theories of collective decision-making, either cooperative or noncooperative, to model interactions within the family. In general, the results from bargaining models are different from those of Beckerian centralized power and the neoclassical "as if" treatment, in interesting ways. For example, in the neoclassical model income from all members is assumed to be simply pooled before decision-making begins, while in collective choice models it may make a difference to whom income accrues.[6]

Nash bargaining models with divorce threat points, pioneered by Marjorie McElroy and Mary Jean Horney (1981), and Marilyn Manser and Murray Brown (1980), allow each individual's utility in the unmarried state to affect intra-familial allocations. Formally, in the Nash problem, the couple (called m and f) maximize the product $[U_m - V_m][U_f - V_f]$, where U_i is the utility in the marriage and V_i is the utility in the nonmarried alternative. Some of the more recent contributions to this literature have explored different and sometimes more general formal theories of bargaining. For example, Shelly Lundberg and Robert Pollak (1994) model marriage as a noncooperative game dividing consumption goods between two agents, while François Bourguignon and Pierre-André Chiappori (1992) have recently put forth models of "collective choice" of two partners over allocations of consumption goods, which assume Pareto efficiency but do not impose specific bargaining solutions. Other contributions have stayed within the Nash framework, but have expanded the domain of bargaining. Notburga Ott (1995), for example, looks at intertemporal issues of time allocation and fertility within the Nash framework. This "economics of

---

[6] Becker (1974) assumed full income pooling (under the control of the "altruist"). Becker (1981) allowed that the "altruist" might be constrained to allowing a "beneficiary" to keep at least their own earnings, but did not follow the consequences other than noting that this would bring an end to the "effectiveness" of the "head's" "altruism."

marriage" literature is characterized by the vocabulary of utility, preferences, and choice, and a high degree of mathematical formalization.

Are these models more feminist than the others? Inasmuch as these collective models include the adult women in the family as people – as agents in their own right – they are certainly a substantial step in the right direction. While commonly billed as "household" or "family" models, however, in practice they are models of marital couples. Children are either invisible in the formal models (e.g., Chiappori 1988), or treated as goods (e.g., Manser and Brown 1980). This may be partly due to the lesser tractability of such models when the number of agents is greater than two. But it is also, as suggested in Samuelson's remark, due to the implausibility of treating infants and children as the rational, autonomous agents who are the only residents allowed (so far) into the economist's modeling world. If we persist in characterizing people as people only insomuch as they can be seen as autonomous agents – requiring that the world be fitted into our norms of methodological individualism – our modeling stops here.

Such models reflect, at best, only half a view of family economic relations. These models start by positing the existence of autonomous agents, and then seek to explain how they come to agree to form a marriage and how they decide to split the benefits then gained. But where do these autonomous agents come from? In adopting a model of autonomous agents as our starting point, we take the Hobbesian view of humans who spring up like mushrooms (see Chapter 2). But people do not spring up like mushrooms. Individuals form families, it is true, but families are also the starting-point for the formation of individuals – through birth, nurturance, and education. Nor do people stay independent forever: illness and age take their toll. More particularly, it has always been women who give birth, and it has historically been women who have borne the bulk of the responsibility for nurturance and education of children, and the care of the sick and elderly. A view of families that focuses only on the prime-age adults makes invisible exactly those activities that have traditionally been of foremost importance to women. Such activities are considered unimportant, part of "nature," and not amenable to study. The decision to study only one side of families – the joining together of adult individuals – without studying the other side – the nurturance of children and care of the elderly – reflects a prejudice that what is not perceived as so important by prime-age men is not so important for scholarship.

The limits of models

To many economists, the families are considered to have an "economic" aspect exactly to the extent that they can be analyzed by using particular modeling techniques. As Gary Becker put it in *The Economic Approach to Human Behavior*, "what most distinguishes economics as a discipline from other disciplines in the social sciences in not its subject matter but its approach" (1976: 5). Becker (1976) identified the core of the "economic approach" as the assumptions of maximizing behavior, market equilibrium, and stable preferences.

One can argue that formal choice-theoretic models of families, such as those discussed in the last section, are given undue weight in the field without denying that they may be clever, mathematically elegant, and sometimes enlightening. Some of the models are brilliant. The problem is not that the models abstract from reality, since all analytical thinking involves some such abstraction. Nor can it always be claimed that the models are empirically untestable or irrelevant to policy. The problem lies in the hegemony of these models in defining the field. If we understand economics as a science, as I assume we do, then the proper role of modeling is to further the understanding of the phenomenon under study. Yet the "economic approach" (in Becker's sense) turns this around, and puts the subject at the service of the axioms and method. The proper role of families, one might surmise, is to provide further ground for the application of the axioms of maximizing behavior. The aspects of marriage and family that do not fit easily into this framework are absorbed into the constraints or simply ignored. At the end of writing or reading an article in this literature, we will certainly, if the article is high quality, know more about how the mathematical maximization model can be stretched and prodded. But how much more will we know about marriage?

Since gaining knowledge about marriage and families does not seem to be the driving force in the formal choice-theoretic approach, one might wonder why such an approach is accorded such high prestige in the profession. Some economists – most notably Becker and some of his followers – believe the world really works in the way described by this model. Most economists in my acquaintance, however, express a preference for such modeling not because they believe it is literally true, but because they perceive it as somehow more rigorous than the alternatives. Deriving conclusions by strict logical deduction from first principles gives one a satisfying impression of coherence. As discussed in earlier chapters, however, feminist scholars have pointed out how the denigration of verbal, analogical, or less formal reasoning as nonreasoning, or at best degraded logic, reflects a certain epistemological "machismo."

Perhaps a reader might feel that the tremendous human capital investment among economists in the techniques of formal modeling means, *per se*, that there is social benefit to continuing this work. This ignores an insight from basic microeconomics: sunk costs are sunk costs, and should not prevent the reallocation of resources into fields more productive at the margin.

By contrasting the narrow formal approach to the economics of marriage and family to more flexible, reasoned, and richer approaches, I will (on pages 74–6) point out specific instances where unclear thinking is permitted, if not caused, by rigid adherence to the path of maximization and formal testing.

NOTES TOWARDS A NEW FEMINIST THEORY

Feminist economists have made, and will probably continue to make headway in developing new models on family and women's issues within the standard framework of mathematical models of individual rational choice. But many feminists report a "gnawing feeling of dissatisfaction" with standard analysis (Ferber and Birnbaum 1977: 19). Analyzing phenomena fraught with connection to others (e.g., responsibility for children), tradition (e.g., the division of household tasks), and relations of domination (e.g., labor market discrimination) with only the language of individual agency, markets, and choice is very likely to create a feeling of distortion; a feeling that that which is most important has been left out. It is like trying to fit a round peg in a square hole. When the standard framework becomes a Procrustean bed, norms of scientific investigation demand that the framework itself, and not the phenomenon being studied, should do the adjusting.[7]

The formal choice-theoretic framework is not, however, the only game in town. As discussed in Chapter 2, one could look not to method but rather to a subject area that could be loosely described as "provisioning" to define "the economics of the family." The starting-point is not the specification of a formal maximization problem, but rather a set of questions about who gets what and who does what; how decisions about jobs, purchases, and household chores are made within families; how the needs of dependents are provided for; and how laws and the social environment shape the context for those decisions. Such works include, for example, parts of Barbara Bergmann's (1986) work on U.S. women; Amartya Sen's work on marriage as a situation of cooperative conflict (1985); Elaine McCrate's analysis of falling marriage rates (1987); and Nancy Folbre's work on gender norms (1993a, 1994). Many works by sociologists, anthropologists, and demographers also come to mind. Arlie Hochschild's (1989) widely quoted work on the intra-household distribution of labor in the U.S.A. is an example, as are Jan Pahl's (1989) work on British financial arrangements in marriage and Vivianna Zelizer's (1994) work on domestic currencies. Works such as those in

---

[7] The Procrustean bed analogy has also been drawn by Sawhill (1977: 121).

Dwyer and Bruce (1988) focus on households in the Third World. The vocabulary used in this second strain of analysis may include terms such as needs, contributions, well-being, power, control, dependence, freedom, rights, legitimacy, tradition, norms, beliefs, and social constraints. In the best of these works, the subject defines the study, with the theory and methods following. Data, taken from a variety of sources (including legal cases, national mortality tables, and small samples of in-home observations), is used to establish empirical regularities.

Perhaps not surprisingly, this field seems to be led by scholars attuned to the economic position of women. The professional environment of economics is still one in which family matters are generally considered to be too personal and sentimental for economic analysis. While Becker broke ground by considering families to be "economic" in a choice-theoretical sense, the economics of families in a provisioning sense has always been a topic that few women can ignore. Marriage has often been a woman's bread and butter.

The study of families in terms of provisioning need not preclude the use of maximization methods – if they are illuminating to the subject at hand. It does not require throwing over a focus on individual choice in favor of an equally narrow focus on social determinism, nor the replacement of quantitative methods with qualitative ones, nor an abandonment of theory in favor of raw measurement; nor the abandonment of a postulate of purposive behavior, broadly construed. It is not, to put it crudely, an abandonment of Becker-style argumentation in favor of (what we economists think of as) fuzzy-headed sociology. While any study may, if badly done, lapse into ad hocery and vagueness, a good study of this will balance the attention given to the individual and to society, quantitative evidence and qualitative evidence, theoretical progress and empirical progress, rationality and constraints on rationality. The criterion used for choice of method is that of usefulness, rather than one of aesthetics. With no set formula to follow, the researcher must be constantly on the watch for fuzzy-headed thinking of all varieties.

I suggest three ways in which feminist theories might significantly broaden the usual economic treatment of the family: using a concept of identity as persons-in-relation, focusing on family behavior as a process, and broadening the domain of "bargaining" to include agency, affiliation, and the standard of living.

A concept of identity as persons-in-relation

In the models of the family discussed above, family members are identified either as independent, autonomous individuals, or as passive nonpersons who can be subsumed into someone else's preferences or into the constraints. The models of the family thus reflect the distorted conception of human identity discussed in Chapter 1, with independence or "separation" linked to adult men and dependence or "connection" associated with everyone else.

How does the family look, if instead we consider each member as both an individual, and as a person embedded in relationships? Instead of a sharp split between agenic adults (or adult males) and nonperson children (or women-and-children), we can envision a continuum of separation and connection. Young children are individuals, in having welfare levels and preferences and at least some limited area of agency, but much of their welfare and activity (and even to some extent their formation of preferences) is determined by their dependence on their parents. As children age, their individuation becomes stronger, their dependence less strong, and they gain more responsibilities towards their siblings and parents. Identity during active parenting years may be primarily characterized by individuation and responsibility, while in old age or illness dependence may again become a primary characteristic.

Such a conception involves at least two dialectical concepts foreign to standard, individual-choice, economic models: economic responsibility and economic dependence. Questions of responsibility come up in discussions of childcare, of financial provisioning, of child support or spousal support, in the allocation of household tasks, in the dividing up of decision-making, and in the maintenance of inter-family connections. Responsibility is also related to the concept of power: one can only carry out a responsibility if one has the positive power to do so, and responsibility may also vest one with a certain power over decisions. Dependence takes financial forms, for example in dependence on someone else's money income; physical forms, for example, a dependence on someone else to do one's laundry or feed one as a child; and developmental form, as in the need of an infant for attention and bonding in order to thrive. Dependence is a key concept in discussion of childcare and elder care, child support and visitation, the appropriate treatment of the family in income taxation (Chapter 7), and the efficacy of family-based programs to raise child welfare. Along with dependence, one might introduce the concept of vulnerability: to be dependent means to rely on someone else's power.

In fact it is hard to say anything intelligent about families without bringing in the concepts of responsibility and dependence, and in fact in standard economics articles complete avoidance of the terms is rare. In such articles, however, these issues are usually quickly treated by recourse to stylized facts or extreme simplifying assumptions, and then dismissed (so that the analysis of the "real" model can proceed), rather than being investigated. But is this the best way to investigate what is happening in the family? To what extent do such models illuminate how families actually operate, instead of simply illuminating how individual-choice models operate?

A feminist theory of families would not treat the traditional allocation of all financial responsibility to the father and all family care responsibilities to the mother as either "natural" or normatively significant. While a mother's relationship of responsibility to a child during pregnancy and lactation (if chosen) cannot be shared, feminists generally feel that extrapolating this to a full eighteen years of sole responsibility for nurturance of a child, plus sole responsibility for the ill and the elderly, is extreme, and harmful. It is harmful to the woman, whose own individuation is jeopardized; to the child who may be encouraged to stay dependent too long, and be made to carry the (unjust) burden of feeling responsible for giving meaning to her or his mother's life; to the father whose skills in relationship are left undeveloped. While some economists have explained the breadwinner–homemaker structure as economically optimal due to gains from specialization, feminists are more likely to point out the disadvantages of specialization: the fatigue that builds up more quickly when there is no variety to tasks, the long-run costs of staying out of the labor force, and the financial vulnerability of the stay-at-home spouse (Ferber and Birnbaum 1977, 1980). Nancy Folbre and Heidi Hartmann (1988) pointed out the contradiction involved in assuming agents are perfectly self-interested in the market, and perfectly "altruistic" at home.

The notion of "altruism," as economists have conceived it, while it may play a role, is not as central a concept to feminist theorizing as are responsibility and dependence. "Altruism" describes a case where I might act in ways that benefit you, because your welfare or your consumption are arguments in my utility function. But this assumes that my utility function is well defined in the absence of all social connection, and that I will only do good to you if I "prefer" to do so, and it makes me better off. Responsibility, on the other hand, means that actions may be taken quite apart from personal preference. Amartya Sen (1982) has discussed this same notion of "persons-in-relation" and the contrast between "altruism" and "responsibility," in his discussion of humans as "social animals" who may act both from "sympathy" and "commitment." Sympathy or altruism moves one to act if another's misfortune makes one feel personally worse off. Commitment or responsibility moves one to act even if the action will bring about no personal gain. If you get up in the middle of the night to feed a baby because you feel sorry for it, you are acting altruistically. If you get up when you would feel personally better off just putting your pillow over your head, you are acting responsibly. Since after the hundredth or so such occasion one is likely to feel more sorry for oneself than for the child, it is a good thing for children that most parents treat childrearing as a commitment.[8] Sympathy or altruism is easily incorporated into standard models by the mechanism of interdependent utility functions; commitment or responsibility violates the underlying separative individualism and hedonism of such models.

A focus on family behavior as process

The standard model of individual utility maximization posits close, deterministic, and frictionless relationships among the predetermined preferences of the unitary agent, the choices the agent makes, and the utility outcome of these choices. The concept of "responsibility" or "commitment" has already thrown one wrench into this well-oiled machine, at the link between personal preferences and choice. Consideration of the multiplicity of persons within a family and the interdependent technology of household living (Nelson 1988) further complicates the analysis. We infer from the fact that every household does locate itself somewhere, and save a certain amount, and that members are observed to buy and sell certain things, that there have in fact been some decisions made. But the decision-making process, that is so simple in the standard individual case (a static and instantaneous "choose so as to maximize utility") that it is taken for granted and rarely discussed, is central to understanding families.

Modeling family decisions as "social choice" problems, in stark contrast to the individual choice problems of unitary agents, may be another false dichotomy. The concept of persons-in-relation means that, while persons have agency, they are also fundamentally influenced by those around them. Consider, as the opposite end of a continuum whose other pole is the modeling of social family behavior as individual (i.e. the subsuming of family behavior under the umbrella of a single neoclassical agent or a Beckerian "head"), how individual choice might be modeled as inherently social. Who has not heard two voices in their head, one telling them to eat some cake and the other telling them that it is unhealthy? What parent has not, at some time, heard their own parent's voice emanating from their own mouth? Do mature and responsible persons never, in considering their own pleasures to be gained from some activity, also consider what others might have to say about it?

---

[8] It should be noted that commitment does not require, and in fact forbids, that one go from the one extreme of neglect to the opposite extreme of self-sacrifice. Responsible adult behavior in the example of nighttime infant feeding includes taking action to encourage a child to sleep through the night, and may even involve ignoring some cries if the effects of sleep deprivation go beyond inconvenience and threaten the parent's health or daytime competence. The self-sacrificing adult who simply reacts to any and all demands, regardless of cost, is guilty of being irresponsible to at least one human being in her (or his) care: herself (or himself).

Even within a person, conversations, conflict and compromise go on. What happens in families may be qualitatively more of the same, but external rather than internalized.[9]

What determines which voice will prevail, in the individual or in the family? With no clear, single utility function to be maximized, "rational choice" is not a very satisfactory answer. Rationality of procedures – for example, systematic ways of letting each voice be heard – may be more relevant than the idea of rationality in choice itself. The central contribution of bargaining models has been to bring attention to some specific factors that may play a role in the decision-making process: in the case of Nash divorce threat models of marriage, the well-being of each spouse in the alternative state of being unmarried; more generally, as outlined in Sen (1985), the factors of fall-back positions and threats.

Sen (1990), however, also suggests that bargaining models have missed three important aspects of what he calls "cooperative conflicts." How much each actor is perceived to be contributing to the relationship may be important. Sen's notion of "perceived contribution" is of special importance to a feminist theory of the family, as a way of incorporating the hypotheses that some of women's disadvantage within patriarchal families may come from a denigration of their contributions – a perception of their contributions being worth less than men's simply because they are made by women. The extent to which each actor perceives concern for his or her own welfare as legitimate is a second important factor. Sen's notion of "perceived legitimacy" allows incorporation of the observation that some women may be so oppressed or overidentified with others as not to express dissatisfaction with their own obvious oppression. The third factor of "cooperative conflicts" that does not fit in the standard bargaining framework is the dynamic issue of how outcomes in one period may affect outcomes later on or even for future generations. The idea of dynamics allows discussion of how traditions are formed, followed, and perhaps changed. A feminist theory may find much to build on in Sen's concepts.

Agency, affiliation, and the standard of living

Standard models of marital bargaining assume that all outcomes may be measured in a single dimension, that of "utilities" of the partners. Consider, instead, the economy of marriage as involving three dimensions: living standards, agency, and affiliation. Living standards refers to

---

[9] Amartya Sen's (1982) model of "meta-rankings" generates something of this type of internal dialog. Howard Margolis (1982) presents a model in which each person contains two (specifically defined) selves. Henry J. Aaron characterizes internal decision-making as "a kind of mad Keystone Kops scramble" (1994: 17).

the paradigmatic arguments of standard economics: the welfare one gets from goods and the use of one's time. Agency is the ability of each person to recognize and promote his or her interests. Affiliation represents the need of human beings to belong and to be loved.

In marital çompromises one may observe deals being struck that trade off one factor for another, sometimes to extremes. "I will take care of all your material needs, as long as you pledge me obedience," goes the trade of living standards for agency freedom between the upper-class husband and his wife, in many cultures. Or, since actual and current arrangements are more complex than implied by that one cultural image, one might see living standards and agency freedom offered in place of affiliation: "Here's the checkbook, now don't bother me." Or see affiliation and agency offered in place of living standards: "I will love you and let you do what you want, but don't expect me to hold a job." Or one may observe living standards rewards for affiliation achievement, say in a polygamous society where the deal is "The wife who bears the most sons gets the biggest house."

It may be argued, of course, that one form of marital structure may dominate because of its superior efficiency, thus simplifying the structure of the problem in need of economic analysis. In the "traditional" marriage (i.e., traditional in selected Western cultures and classes) the husband specializes in agency, as demonstrated in personal achievements in the market and as well as chief decision-maker status at home, and the wife in affiliation, demonstrated by caring and nurturing activities, as well as a willingness to bend to another's will. In such a household, agency and affiliation issues are apparently forever solved, and the problem for the social scientist reduces (conveniently) to that of the standard of living. Yet casual observation suggests that the presumed benefits of such specialization may be far overrated. Women in particular have, in large numbers, "voted with their feet" in favor of lives with increased agency freedom, even if this means still shouldering all the affiliation tasks as well. One may want to treat with skepticism those attempts to sanction the highly specialized marital structure as natural, or as most economically efficient.

It is certainly at least as plausible to posit that marriages in which the spouses each explore a wider range of "doing and being" (Sen 1984) have welfare-enhancing properties that outweigh any losses from lessened specialization. Such couples are likely to have more joint interests and be better able to understand and empathize with each other's problems. It may be less burdensome for each individual to have a broad range of responsibilities, shared, than a narrow range entirely on one's own shoulders. At the level of activities, this may arise from a simple preference for variety in daily tasks, or from the advantages of diversification as a form of insurance in the face of uncertainty about future job opportunities, marital status, health, etc. One might even argue that a partner who resists developing agency, or resists developing affiliation, is settling for a form of "being" that is suboptimal. I doubt that many people would regard the "Here's the checkbook, now don't bother me" marriage as exemplary.

While standard of living, agency, and affiliation issues may form the base of marital "cooperative conflicts," sometimes one issue may come to the fore. For example, standard of living issues may be highlighted for study in countries and classes where lives are lived on the margin, so that discrimination against wives in healthcare and nutrition can have mortal consequences. Yet even a passing familiarity with the literature on women and development suggests that agency issues, such as the right to hold an outside job and control one's earnings, and affiliation issues, such as the capability of controlling fertility and the ramifications of divorce law, play crucial roles in the economics of marriage. In the contemporary United States, I would suggest that the area of most social conflict, and of most interest for social science research, is the affiliation question of who is responsible, in time and in money, for children. Much research (e.g., reviewed in Bergmann 1986) suggests the stylized fact that wives' increased agency has been permitted, not so much by husbands taking on affiliative work, but by decreases in wives' standards of living, particularly in regard to time for rest and recreation.

While these variables of standard of living, agency, and affiliation go beyond the narrow economic variables of income use (and, slightly broader, time use), they clearly have implications for such more narrowly defined distributions. It is not necessary in every study that one should explicitly take into account all dimensions, and that one should go into all individual households to investigate all possible permutations of distribution. However, it is necessary that one should understand the way in which the part one wants to study is part of a larger context, and how legal, cultural, bureaucratic, and market forces can influence not only the perceived "terms of trade," but the perceived legitimacy of the trade itself.

THE PERILS OF MISPLACED SCIENTIFICITY

Instead of using such richer models, economists have tended to focus on marriage and families only to the extent that they can be captured within a choice-theoretic model. The axioms of maximization and the methods of mathematical derivation are allowed to direct the development of analysis. Such procedure opens, not closes, the door to muddy thinking, misspecification, and poor analytical procedure.

First, there is a problem of confusing issues by mislabeling. Becker's work on "altruism," for example, muddied the waters by segueing from a sentimental, affiliation-oriented verbal explanation, to a formalization in which agency issues (power) are arguably the more central. Similarly, the treatment of children as "goods" in a parental utility function, on a par with beer and pretzels, puts a living standards label on an issue with strong affiliation components. Certainly there are times in which considering the influence children have on their parents' standard of living is appropriate, such as in the case where children provide security for old age in the absence of social pensions. Yet, as I will trace in the next chapter, the image of children as arguments in adult utility functions has generated considerable confusion in parts of the economics literature.

Second, there is a problem of misplaced concreteness. For example, while the literature on marital bargaining or "collective choice" makes some headway over the "altruist" model in allowing for some discussion of agency (in that there are two agents, instead of one) and affiliation (negatively, in models that refer to divorce threats), the domain of the bargain is usually vastly underspecified. If, as argued above, marital bargaining goes on, on many different levels and with strong outside influence, mathematical tractability of theoretical (that is, thoughtful and analytical) formulations is likely to be the exception rather than the rule. Once one has forced tractability of the problem of intra-household allocation by getting rid of the problem of responsibility for childcare by assigning it to the mother in the assumptions (as in Lundberg and Pollak 1993), or forced tractability by reducing the dimensionality of the joint decision-making problem all the way back to consumption and "leisure" (with no mention of household production, as in Chiappori 1988), is it really so interesting just what functional form the allocation takes, or what the properties of the joint Slutsky matrix are?

Choice of solution concepts may also mask implicit restrictions about the domain of bargaining. While the often used Nash solution gives a marriage model a comforting closure, the Nash solution is the unique solution only when one requires that the bargaining game also satisfy a set of restrictive axioms. The axiom of symmetry with respect to the roles of the players underlying the Nash solution is a significant restriction of the possible agency (or differential power) relationships between the two players. Take-it-or-leave-it offers by one agent, for example, are ruled out. While many mainstream economists seem to find the possible indeterminacy of many real world bargaining problems unsettling, feminists and postmodernists (Seiz 1991; Mehta 1993) are more likely to see this as a problem with economists rather than a problem with the world. While the solving out of a difficult model may give one a great feeling of satisfaction and accomplishment, that feeling may be all that is produced.

The use of overly restrictive assumptions in the service of tractability points to another problem as well. At some point we shift away from the investigation of the phenomenon, towards what Donald McCloskey (1991) has called the "search through the hyperspace of assumptions": "If you build a model showing X, I can refute you by choosing different assumptions and showing Y." Formalism certainly has a valid role in science when it protects against logical error, but if all that is done is the comparing of one logical construct to another, we demonstrate a very poor understanding of the larger analytical process.

HOW DO WE KNOW WHEN WE HAVE A THEORY?

A reader of this chapter may feel misled: the title promised some moves towards a feminist theory of the family, but the chapter up to this point presents no model of utility maximization, no first-order conditions, no comparative statics or dynamic results. No apologies are offered. Formal models can help clarify the subject, illuminate unforeseen conclusions, and protect against errors of logic, but they do not in themselves constitute all of theory. I have heard it suggested that economic theories fall in tripartite categories: theories about the world, theories about theories, and theories about math. While most economists working on household behavior have (by at least giving some context to their "agents") avoided a wholesale move into theories about math, much of the literature has remained concentrated at the level of theories about theories. We take the standard neoclassical theory of individual choice, and push and prod it into illustrating something that might occur in actual families. Perhaps we build a model that is consistent with a stylized fact, or come up with one possible way of interpreting results from econometric analysis. And then we often stop.

The problem is not that we work with such models. The problem is that we are too often content with formalization *per se* and with a single model, and never move on to the next steps required for a science: showing that, in fact, the formalization aids our understanding (in ways significantly beyond what we could get from verbal reasoning alone); and showing that our model performs better than alternative "consistent" models when these are all put up against the full range of the data. Should we take more seriously this last challenge, we might find we need new types of data, and we may find that the formal models of rational individual choice are less helpful than we expected, especially in their most sophisticated forms.[10] If we are willing to drop our

---

[10] Marjorie McElroy (1990), for example, makes a distinction between the "practical and fundamental" contributions of the Nash bargaining model, and its "more sophisticated but less fundamental and less practical implications." She makes an analogy to the neoclassical model: the symmetry and negativity conditions for the neoclassical substitution matrix are less useful than the theory's other implications, and also are not often confirmed in empirical work.

androcentric biases, we can search for better theories about the world. Feminists can certainly continue to work within the accepted frameworks of thought, but the returns from using a broader-based theory may be higher.

Real economic problems of families need attention from economic analysts. Economists want to know how families work. As a society, this knowledge is needed in order to decide how better to alleviate child poverty, how to tax families fairly and efficiently, and how to encourage equity within families, including between the sexes. To gain this knowledge most efficiently, economists should be willing to expand the toolbox to new theories and methods, when old ones prove inadequate. Such discussion assumes, of course, that economists' loyalty is to learning about the world through the practice of social science. If this is incorrect – if the profession's primary loyalty is to the old theories *per se* – then one must ask if the profession has degenerated from scientific practice into merely an exercise in stylized mental gymnastics.

6

HOUSEHOLD EQUIVALENCE SCALES: THEORY VS. POLICY?

A MORE DETAILED EXAMPLE

The previous chapter argued that formal, rational choice modeling should not be allowed to direct economists' research into issues of marriage and family. This chapter illustrates, in greater historical and technical depth, exactly how an increasingly narrow focus on individual (instead of interdependent) agents and on mental (as contrasted to standard-of-living) conceptions of utility has created distortions in one specific area of research. The reader unfamiliar with formal consumer theory may skim the more technical parts of the discussion – or even skip this entire chapter – without much loss in continuity.

How much more does a family of four need than a family of two, to be just as well off? Household equivalence scales measure the relative income needs of households of different sizes and composition. Expressed as ratios, they answer the question of how much income different households would need to attain the same welfare level. Myriad policy decisions depend implicitly or explicitly on sets of equivalence scales; myriad papers have been published by economists about the theory and estimation of such scales. Unfortunately for policy use, the policy and the academic interests have increasingly diverged. While the general definition of household equivalence scales uses the terms "household" and "welfare," distinct definitions have been given to these key terms. Older theory and most policy applications define "household welfare" as the material standard of living of every individual in the household (including the children). The bulk of current academic literature defines "household welfare" as the material standard of living of the adults or parents in the household. And a view increasingly gaining ground defines "household welfare" as the subjective utility (i.e., overall happiness) of the adults or parents.

Table 6.1 1992 weighted average poverty thresholds

(1) *Size of* *family unit*	(2) *Poverty* *guideline* $	(3) *Implicit scale* *(base = single* *Person)*	(4) *Implicit scale* *(base = family of* *four)*
1	7,143	1.0	0.50
2	9,137	1.28	0.64
3	11,186	1.57	0.78
4	14,335	2.01	1.0
5	16,952	2.37	1.18
6	19,137	2.68	1.34
7	21,594	3.02	1.51
8	24,053	3.37	1.68

Source: United States Department of Commerce, 1993: A-2. The thresholds actually used in statistical calculation allow for 48 different combinations of family size, number of children, and age of householder.

HOUSEHOLD EQUIVALENCE SCALES IN USE

As an example of a prominent use of household equivalence scales, consider the poverty income thresholds used by the U.S. Department of Commerce, Bureau of the Census, in measuring the incidence of poverty in the United States. Weighted-average summaries of the guidelines used in analyzing data gathered in March 1993 are given in column (2) of Table 6.1. Such a schedule explicitly sets out the amounts of money income assumed to be required by households of different size to reach the same welfare level, in this case, a borderline poverty standard of living. Columns (3) and (4) give the implicit household equivalence scales on single-person and four-person household bases, respectively. For example, the poverty line standard says that a five-person household is considered to need 18 per cent more income than a four-person household, and 137 per cent more than a one person household, to be just out of poverty. Closely related poverty guidelines are issued by the Department of Health and Human Services (HHS), for use in deciding eligibility for numerous federal programs including Food Stamps, school lunches, Head Start, WIC (Women, Infants, Children supplemental food program), Job Corps and many Job Training and Partnership Act programs, some aspects of Medicaid, Community Services block grants, Maternal and Child Health block grants, and Legal Services. (Fischer 1991 Federal Register 1994).[1] State and local agencies may choose to use the HHS guidelines, or may create their own (usually implicit)

[1] For 1994, the HHS poverty guidelines (for all states but Alaska and Hawaii) were equal to $7,360 for one person, plus $2,480 for each additional person. (Federal Register 1994).

equivalence scales, in setting eligibility and payment levels for the programs they administer.

Moving beyond comparisons at only the poverty standard of living, equivalence scales play a role in more general investigations of income distribution. It is generally thought that total household income is a poor indicator of household welfare since it will tend to show large households as better off than they actually are. The next simplest measure, per capita income, overcorrects for household size and understates the welfare of larger households, since larger households may include more children (who are usually presumed to have lower needs than adults) and may benefit from household economies of scale in consumption. Household equivalence scales designed by official agencies such as the Bureau of Labor Statistics (BLS), the Organization for Economic Cooperation and Development (OECD), or the European Union have been used more generally to adjust measures of income inequality for household size (Buhmann *et al.* 1988). One gets a different measure of inequality, and a different picture of who is at the top and bottom of the income distribution, depending on the adjustment used.

What are the basic conceptions underlying these policy-related uses of household equivalence scales? The comparison of "welfare" levels in terms of income adjusted for household size implies that the welfare notion is one of "material," "financial," or "economic" welfare. The critical question is what level of consumption of goods and services people are able to afford, not what level of overall happiness they may happen to attain. Also implicit in the design of these scales is the idea that within the household, welfare levels are equalized. All members of a household that is in poverty are usually considered poor, and all members of households out of poverty are usually considered non-poor (see, for example, U.S. House of Representatives 1985; U.S. Department of Commerce 1993). While such an assumption may lead one easily to substitute between references to "household," "parental," or "child" welfare, the policy uses to which these scales are put suggest that child welfare may even be of special concern. Four of the programs mentioned above that use the HHS guidelines are especially directed towards children. It is a rare discussion of poverty that does not include some reference to the special vulnerability of children in poverty, who are unable to escape poverty by their own efforts, and who may suffer lasting effects on health and intelligence from early deprivation.

How are the equivalence scales used for policy purposes put together? The Census and HHS scales have a common base in work done by Mollie Orshansky in the early 1960s (1965). Orshansky calculated the cost of the USDA "economy food plan" for households of different size and composition, converted this to a measure of income needs by multiplying by a factor taken to represent the cost of nonfood essentials, and finally weighted these according to percentages of different types of households in the population in 1964. Orshansky was careful to point out that the poverty line income guidelines did not rest on the assumption that families would have minimally adequate diets at the poverty line, but only that, with judicious spending, they could. Families with three or more members had their presumed food costs multiplied by three, based on the fact that in 1955 the average proportion of income spent on food was 33 percent. Families of two had their food costs multiplied by a somewhat higher factor to take into account their "relatively larger fixed costs" such as for housing and utilities, while the poverty line for one-person households was created using scales from another agency and further ad hoc adjustments for fixed costs (1965: 9). The Census Bureau statistical poverty thresholds today are, with only minor revisions, these 1964 Orshansky numbers, updated by the Consumer Price Index (U.S. Department of Commerce 1993). The Health and Human Services policy guidelines began on the same basis in 1965, but in 1973 were rounded off for administrative purposes so that each additional person adds the same amount to the poverty level (Fischer 1991; U.S. Department of Commerce 1993). Such simplifications and ad hoc "rules of thumb" also play an important role in other equivalence scales: the OECD scales simply state that the first adult be assigned a value of 1, the second adult a value of 0.7, and children a value of 0.5 in calculating needs-adjusted household size (Ringen 1991).[2]

It has also been suggested that household equivalence scales should be helpful in calculating guidelines for child support awards. Rather than asking the question of equivalent incomes in terms of a ratio, it could be asked in terms of absolute differences in dollars. How much extra income does a household need with the addition of a child? While this approach intuitively gives us an estimate of the "cost of a child" or the expenditures "on" a child, its practical usefulness in designing child support policy is limited. To the extent that households enjoy economies of scale, it is a marginal "cost," rather than total "cost," measure, and is hence conditional on the welfare level enjoyed by, and on the structure of, the reference household. In child support cases, there are at least two reference households to consider: that of the custodial and that of the

---

[2] For an indication of the degree of disagreement between scales in use, see Buhmann *et al.* (1988) or Atkinson and Bourguignon (1989: 12). The latter cite a study that, in surveying existing estimates of equivalence scales, found a single adult to be equivalent to from 49 percent to 94 percent of a couple, and a couple with two children to be from 111 percent to 193 percent of a childless couple.

noncustodial parent. The amount necessary to bring child welfare up to a given level in the household of a parent who is already well off, for example, will probably be quite different from that necessary in a household with an asset-poor parent who has a history of being out of the labor force. While some states have used empirical estimates derived by economists in figuring how much of parental income is spent "on" children, the relationship of these estimates to actual guidelines, according to a recent exhaustive survey (Lewin/ICF 1990: 6–8), is a loose one. Considerations of fairness between parents, parental ability to pay, and parents' ability to meet their own basic needs are also in general given substantial weight in the design of formulas, arrived at through political and administrative negotiation.

The multiplicity of equivalence scales in actual use, and their frequently ad hoc nature, suggests that there could be a role for economic theory in facilitating clear thinking in this area and more reliable estimation of the scales themselves.

EQUIVALENCE SCALE THEORY IN HISTORICAL PERSPECTIVE

Household welfare as the economic welfare of all members

Robert Cooter and Peter Rappoport (1984), in their review of pre- and post-"ordinalist revolution" schools of thought, present evidence that the dominant conception of utility prior to the 1930s was that of material well being. Physical well being "was conceived as nearly equivalent to productive capacity," and hence was directly and objectively observable. "Needs" could be simply defined as deficiencies in meeting the goal of physical health. Interpersonal comparability was not considered a stumbling block, since it was assumed that people were fundamentally alike in physical needs, and comparisons were made in terms of class averages rather than between individuals. Cooter and Rappoport could also have cited numerous examples from the early history of equivalence scales. Taking this physical sense to its mechanical extreme, Ernst Engel in 1895 drew an analogy between the size and weight of a person and the height and diameter of a cylinder. On this basis he assigned numbers of standard units, normalized on an infant being equal to a value of one, to household members and created an early set of household equivalence scales in "quets" (as he named his unit).[3] More common was the use of dietary requirements, that is, the relative food needs determined by dietary studies of persons of different

[3] This is not to be confused with the food share "Engel Method" to be discussed below.

age, sex, health, and activity level. Edgar Sydenstricker and Willford King (1921) for example, built on early USDA studies of caloric needs of other persons relative to a young man in good health doing moderate labor, that is, expressed in "Adult Male Units." They used a variety of other pieces of information to try to generalize these food scales to scales representing all "requirements for the expense of maintenance" (1921: 852). A combination of food scales and information on "customary expenditures" was used by Faith Williams and Alice Hanson (1940) in creating BLS scales for 1934–6. This materialist view and the use of dietary scales did not immediately disappear with the ordinalist revolution in utility theory. Dietary requirements and health outcomes remain among the most used ways of measuring welfare in developing countries (e.g. Haddad and Kanbur 1990; Thomas 1990), and, as was pointed out above, the dietary requirements approach lives on in today's U.S. poverty lines.

Such reasoning involves not only a material definition of welfare, but, as in the policy uses considered above, an assumption that each member of the household will actually have his or her needs met to the same degree. As put by Sydenstricker and King, "One would scarcely expect differences in age and sex to have an effect upon food expenses different from that which they had upon food needs in calories." (1921: 845). By assuming that expenditures change lockstep with relative needs, the "household" welfare level is made synonymous with the welfare level of each and every individual household member. The choice of unit – whether infant-equivalents or single-adult-equivalents or couple-equivalents – is then arbitrary and can be converted without consequence.

While sharing the same basic notion of a common household material welfare standard with the users of dietary scales, another branch of research took a somewhat less mechanical, and more behavioral approach to estimation of equivalence scales. S.J. Prais and H.S. Houthakker (1955: 125–6) wrote that the investigation into the "standard of living of households of different composition" might be better served by looking at "the behavior of households and not a [nutritionist's] prescription as to their optimum behavior." They suggested that the "relative requirements of different types of persons" might be found by iterative estimation of goods-specific scales (showing the relative requirements for each specific good) and the total-expenditure scale (the overall equivalence scale for a group of goods) from expenditure survey data, at least for goods for which economies of scale are unimportant. Unfortunately, the Prais–Houthakker approach suffers from a fundamental problem of underidentification (Muellbauer 1980).

A more popular way of making use of data on household behavior has been to select some observable value as a proxy for household material welfare. Ernst Engel's 1857 statement, "The proportion of the outgo used for food, other things being equal, is the best measure of the material standard of living of a population," has inspired numerous researchers to use the proportion of income spent on food as a proxy for the standard of living of particular households. This has come to be called the "Engel Method" of equivalence scale estimation. The intuition comes from the fact that the food share moves in desirable directions for a household welfare – or, more accurately, "ill-fare" – proxy: it falls with income, holding household size constant, and rises with household size, holding income constant. Such food-share scales have been calculated for the U.S. by the Bureau of Labor Statistics in 1960 and 1968, by Joseph Seneca and Michael Taussig in 1971, and by Thomas Espenshade in 1984, among others.[4] Of course, the share of income spent on food is not the only plausible proxy: the share of income saved (BLS 1948) and the share of income spent on "necessities" (Watts 1967; Seneca and Taussig 1971) have been among the other suggestions. And here lies the rub: each method may produce a different result. Goods shares reflect not only welfare differences among households, but also differences in the needs of the various types of members and differences in the ability to exploit economies of scale. For example, in one recent study (Nelson 1991), food, rent, and fuel were found to be necessities, and apparel, transportation, and household furnishings and operations, luxuries, for any household size. As would be expected by the intuition behind the welfare proxy approach, the share of expenditure going to the necessities food and fuel rose with household size, income held constant, and the share going to the luxuries, transportation and household furnishings dropped. But the share of rent, a necessity, dropped with household size, and the share of apparel, a luxury, remained constant. While this pattern is perfectly reasonable in the light of household economies of scale in consumption of shelter (Nelson 1988) and the higher clothing intensity of children relative to adults (Nelson 1989), equivalence scales based on the goods-share intuition would in these cases have yielded perverse results. Deaton and Muellbauer (1986) have pointed out that if children are relatively food intensive, the food-share method will yield an upward bound to true equivalence scales. With no reason (other than tradition) for preferring one proxy over another, the sheer volume of competing methods may leave one despairing of even comparing the quality of the

---

[4] While Orshansky mentioned the food-share method in the 1965 piece describing the creation of the U.S. poverty line, it was not in fact consistently used there. Consistent application of the food-share approach would have meant multiplying presumed food costs by the same factor for all types of households, instead of allowing for other adjustments for "fixed costs."

various estimates, let alone finding definitive ones, at least without further analytical inquiry.[5]

Household welfare as the economic welfare of the adults

A subtle change in vocabulary, which can be traced at least as far back as the work of Erwin Rothbarth in 1943, substitutes the terms "adult welfare" or "parental welfare" for "household welfare." As Rothbarth put it, the question is "How much additional income does a family *consisting of husband and wife* require to compensate it for the cost of upkeep of a child?" (123; emphasis added). Rather than proxying household welfare by the share of income going to food or other necessities, Rothbarth's own proposal was to use the level of "excess income" as a "criterion of the standard of living of the parents" (ibid: 123). While in the original article it is unclear whether Rothbarth is defining "excess income" as luxury expenditure or as expenditure devoted exclusively to adults, it is the latter that has come to be called the "Rothbarth Method."

The use of the terms "household" or "family" to mean a household's adult members has become ingrained in much of the literature on families. In an interesting reinterpretation of history, Engel is almost invariably referred to as the originator of adult-equivalence scales (Gronau 1988) or methods of measuring the welfare of adults (Deaton and Muellbauer 1986), even though, as described above, Engel actually proposed infant-equivalence scales (in 1895) and a method of measuring the welfare of a population (in 1857). Of course, if adult and child welfare are still assumed to move in lockstep, the substitution of "adult

---

[5] Other ways of using household expenditure survey information, besides the Prais–Houthakker and welfare-proxy approaches have also been proposed. Edward Lazear and Robert Michael (1980) attempted their estimation using reduced form demand equations and external estimates of price elasticities, but the concept of "equivalence" applied in that method is not well defined. Other researchers (Turchi 1975; Lindert 1978; Edwards *et al.* 1982) have given in to the temptation to regard the coefficients in demand equations on dummies representing children as representative of expenditures "on" children. However, if income is also on the right-hand side of the estimated equations, some coefficients will be negative and the researcher must apply ad hoc adjustments to get sensible-looking results. Holding income constant, children will increase household purchases of some goods and decrease purchases of others (as pointed out by van der Gaag 1982). A different sort of household survey approach has been suggested by Kapteyn and van Praag (1976). Respondents are asked to state what level of income they would consider "good," "sufficient," "bad," etc. for their household. Equivalence scales are derived by assigning numerical values to these different welfare levels, and using these, the reported income levels, household composition variables, and a specific functional form to summarize the variation in satisfaction with household size. A similar subjective approach has also been used to define poverty lines (Kapteyn *et al.* 1988).

welfare" for "household welfare" may not necessarily imply a lack of concern for child welfare. Rothbarth, for example, assumed that "there will be a broad correspondence between the standard of living attained by the parents and the standard of living of the child." The implications of the substitution of "adult" for "household" must be examined on a case-by-case basis.[6]

In their influential work, Angus S. Deaton and John Muellbauer explicitly focus on parental utility (1986: 724, 742), and suggest that one particular model of adult-oriented household equivalence scales, the "Gorman–Barten Model," "can be regarded as generalizing [both the Engel and Rothbarth models], so that it is a good candidate for a 'true' model against which to evaluate the alternatives." (p. 735). Muellbauer also suggested in an earlier work that the Barten model might be thought of as a generalization of the method of Prais and Houthakker (Muellbauer 1974). The shift to adult welfare, however, means that the model addresses a quite different question than that asked by Engel or Prais and Houthakker. The Gorman–Barten model is not simply agnostic about the welfare level of children, as implied by Deaton and Muellbauer (1986: 742) who state that the assumption of common welfare levels remains "one possible assumption." Instead the model rather implies that, one, substitution possibilities within the structure of adult preferences will cause children to receive relatively less than they would under a proportional "requirements" scheme; and two, that to the extent that children consume goods not consumed by adults, their consumption (and hence welfare) will not rise with household income.

Since this model has received endorsement by Deaton and Muellbauer and considerable attention from others, this point should be elaborated.[7] Recall from the previous chapter that the Barten model can be written as

---

[6] It might be thought that an emphasis on adult material welfare might be applicable, if not to equivalence scale studies, then to fertility studies. This assumes that it is primarily the "cost" of a child in terms of parents' own consumption that enters the parental decisions. But if some of the "costs" of additional children are borne by earlier children (as is likely), and fertility decisions take into account the material welfare of existing and future children as well as parental welfare, we are back at a model that includes child welfare.

[7] The Barten model has been used without criticism by, among others, Fischer (1987), Jorgenson and Slesnick (1987), Blundell (1980), Kakwani (1980), van der Gaag and Smolensky (1982), and Assarsson (1985). Bojer (1977) is a notable exception to this easy acceptance of the model, in commenting on the oddity of identifying household utility with that of only the "head." Nelson (1988) estimates a special case of the Barten model that avoids the perverse effects described in the text: under the very restrictive assumptions that all household members have the same preferences and are treated symmetrically, substitution effects are made impossible and the model is identical to one that could also be derived from a Samuelsonian social welfare function.

$$U = U\left[\frac{Z_1}{m_1(a)}, \frac{Z_2}{m_2(a)}, \ldots, \frac{Z_J}{m_J(a)}\right] \tag{1}$$

where $U[\cdot]$ is the parents' utility function over their own consumption of goods $j = 1, \ldots, J$, the Z_j are total household purchases of the goods, and the functions $m_j(\cdot)$ are goods-specific equivalence scales that depend on a, a vector describing household composition. The Z_j / m_j terms represent "the consumption of good $[j]$ that actually reaches the parents when an amount $[Z_j]$ is purchased for the family as a whole" (Deaton and Muellbauer 1986). For example, m_j is equal to one if children do not consume the good (or if the good is entirely public within the household), equal to two if parents get one half of total household purchases, etc. The m_j are all equal to one in the household of a childless couple. As the $m_j(\cdot)$ functions are assumed to be dictated from outside the household, and to be invariant to changes in income or prices, they have the nature of expressing the relative "requirements" for families of different sizes with respect to specific goods (Muellbauer 1977: 469), much as in the older dietary scale literature.

The dual of this utility function is the minimization of a cost function defined over parental utility and modified prices,

$$c = c[U, p_1 m_1(a), p_2 m_2(a), \ldots, p_J m_J(a)] \tag{2}$$

From this form comes the interpretation that "the presence of children alters the effective prices of parental consumption" (Deaton and Muellbauer 1986: 736), as was pointed out in the Chapter 5 discussion of the Barten model. One of Gorman's (1976) suggested modifications of the Barten model was the addition of "overheads." Interpreting these as "fixed costs of children," Deaton and Muellbauer include this modification in order to account for household purchases of items that are not naturally part of a childless couple's utility function (like diapers or baby foods). The Gorman–Barten model is thus

$$c = c[U, p_1 m_1(a), p_2 m_2(a), \ldots, p_J m_J(a)] + \sum_i p_i b_i(a) \tag{3}$$

When data on prices are available in addition to data on household composition and consumption patterns, (Gorman–)Barten-type demand equations may be estimated, and expenditure functions recovered by integration (as long as the integrability conditions hold, and one believes in the correctness of the posited functional form). Then general household equivalence scales (m_0) can be constructed by taking the ratio of the expenditure function for any household (h) at reference utility levels and prices to the expenditure function for the reference childless household (R) at the same utility level and prices (Muellbauer 1977):

$$m_0(U, p, a^b) = \frac{c(U, p, a^b)}{c(U, p, a^R)}$$

$$= \frac{c[U, p_1 m_1(a^b), p_2 m_2(a^b), \ldots, p_J m_J(a^b)] + \sum_i p_i b_i(a^b)}{c^R(U, p)} \qquad (4)$$

(remembering that all goods-specific scales are equal to one for the reference household).

While the works by Barten, Gorman, Deaton, and Muellbauer certainly advanced the use of modern consumer theory in the definition of equivalence scales, the focus on adult utility has also led to confusion in areas where the old and new understandings of equivalence scales do not overlap. In particular, the way in which the normalization of the m_j parameters on *adult couple* equivalence breaks with the earlier tradition, when incorporated into a general utility function in which substitution effects are allowed, seems to have gone largely unnoticed. In the early models, up to and including the Prais–Houthakker model, the normalization would have been unimportant: the choice between child equivalents and adult equivalents as the unit of measure could be arbitrary. In the Barten model the normalization is critically important: normalizing $m_j = 1$ for the childless couple household (or single adult male household – see Muellbauer 1974 or Chapter 5), means that the basic utility function by which relationships of substitutability and complementarity are defined is that of the adults, defined over their own consumption. The idea that adults can substitute among commodities – i.e. that since "having children makes ice cream, milk and soft drink relatively more expensive and makes whiskey or cigarettes relatively cheaper" (Deaton and Muellbauer 1980), adults will substitute away from the former goods towards the latter – eliminates the idea that allocation according to goods-specific equivalence scales will equally (or at least proportionally) satisfy the needs of the various persons in the household.

This implication can be illustrated with a very simple example. If Leontief preferences are assumed for adults, the Barten model is similar to the Prais–Houthakker approach. Suppose that goods-specific equivalence scales for two private goods are determined according to the amount of each that an adult and a child would need for each to reach a designated welfare level, under the assumption of Leontief preferences for the adults, $U^A = min(Z_1/m_1, Z_2/m_2)$. For example, assume that a child is "0.8 of an adult" in consumption of good 1 (e.g. milk) and does not consume good 2 (e.g. beer), and that there are equal numbers of adults and children in the household. With a household income of \$10, and prices normalized at one, it can be directly solved that the adults will consume \$3.57 of milk and \$3.57 of beer, while the children reach the same utility level ($u^C = (1/.8)Z_1^C$) with a consumption of \$2.86 of milk. The Barten model in general, however, allows reallocation of the household budget purely according to the adults' preferences between milk and beer and with no regard for reallocation at the adults/children margin. Suppose that instead of Leontief indifference curves between milk and beer, the adults have a Cobb-Douglas utility function: then the household consumption vector will be $Z_1^A = 5$, $Z_2^A = 2.78$, and $Z_1^C = 2.22$. It can be easily shown that the adults' welfare has risen at the expense of the children's. It can also be easily shown that the intra-household allocation is Pareto-inferior: the adults could increase their own utility without taking a higher share of income by reallocating their expenditures on themselves evenly between milk and beer. If it happens that the adults find beer and milk to be perfect substitutes, they will spend $10 on beer and the children will get nothing at all.

Modifying the Barten model by adding the Gorman "fixed costs," while at least assuring some positive expenditure on child-specific goods, does not help in recovering the old assumption of common intra-household welfare levels. As the quantity of purchases of diapers, etc., are assumed to be independent of prices and income (see equation (3)), children's consumption of child-specific goods is assumed to remain fixed as household income rises.

Like the Gorman–Barten model, an intertemporal model recently proposed by Banks et al. (1991) also defines "household welfare" in such a way as to obscure consideration of children. Their model is one of life-cycle consumption under the assumption of perfect capital markets. The definition of a "household" life cycle is in general ambiguous, since there are not one but many different life spans represented in a multiperson household. Banks et al. choose as their relevant life cycle the lifespan of the household "head." Just as the Gorman–Barten model allows substitution away from goods needed by children, so their model allows substitution away from expenditure in periods when children are in the household. "Households are encouraged to substitute expenditure away from periods with children if the elasticity of substitution is large enough, and this could, in theory, be sufficiently extreme to mean that expenditure paths may actually *dip* as children enter the household" (Banks et al. 1991: 22; emphasis in original).

While the literature on adult-oriented equivalence scales has added theoretical rigor and consideration of both intra- and inter-temporal substitution possibilities to the discussion of equivalence scales, there is a fundamental discrepancy between the structure of Gorman–Barten and the Banks–Blundell–Preston intertemporal models and the questions posed in the earlier historical and policy contexts. If households really do act in these ways, then policy questions that assume rough equivalence of welfare within the household need radical reformulation (in very specific directions); if on the other hand households (and policy-makers) really do consider the welfare of children directly in making consumption decisions, these models can hardly provide good guidelines.

The problem of incongruence between method and policy in these cases lies in the specification of household utility as adult utility, not in the choice-theoretic formalization *per se*. In the case of recent utility-theoretic expressions of the Rothbarth (adult-goods) model, the assumption that only adult welfare matters is relatively innocent, and could easily be dispensed with. Gronau (1988), for example, shows that the level of expenditure on goods consumed only by adults will be a correct indicator of household welfare if "parents' welfare" can be described by the following separable function over their utility from their own consumption U^A and their utility from their children's consumption, U^C:

$$U = f[U^A, U^C] \tag{5}$$

One could easily reinterpret U^C as a measure of the children's own material welfare, and reinterpret U as an index of household welfare coming from a "mini social choice problem" (Samuelson 1956; Sen 1984: 378) over adult and child material welfare levels, and thus move away from the adult-only focus.[8] Unfortunately, one condition for this household function to be separable, and thus for the Rothbarth model to hold empirically, is the unlikely one of no household public goods.[9] Another choice-theoretic approach, pursued by Ray (1983), treats the household as a "black box" with a single utility function, and estimates equivalence scales directly. Letting $m_0(U, p, a^b)$ denote a "general equivalence scale" that may depend on prices and the welfare level of comparison, as well as on household composition, the cost function of any household (h) is written as a function of this and the cost function of the reference household (R):

$$c(U, p, a^b) = m_0(U, p, a^b) \, c^R(U, p) \tag{6}$$

With suitable specification of functional forms for $m_0(\cdot)$ and $c^R(\cdot)$, estimation from household demand data is possible.[10] While this equation is

---

[8] Deaton and Muellbauer's (1986: 737) notion that the Gorman–Barten method generalizes the Robarth method relies on an assumption that the Rothbarth model requires that children generate only "fixed," and not income-variable, costs: ("note that, with all m_i's unity but nonzero [fixed costs], the Rothbarth procedure is correct"). The Rothbarth method in general does not impose this restriction.

[9] The empirical plausibility of separability between adult and child consumption has been investigated by Deaton *et al.* (1989), Gronau (1991), and Nelson (1991a).

[10] Estimated in Ray (1983). A variant of this approach was also suggested by Lewbel (1989) and Blackorby and Donaldson (1991) who make the additional assumption that $m_0(\cdot)$ is independent of the level of utility. (Lewbel called this assumption "Independent of Base," while Blackorby and Donaldson called it "Equivalence Scale Exactness"). Estimation of this restricted model was attempted by Phipps (1991) and Nelson(1993a), in spite of recognition of the problem of identification.

simply a rearrangement of the first line of equation (4), direct estimation of $m_0(\cdot)$ avoids the Barten (bottom line of equation (4)) problem of modeling children as quasi-price effects in their parents' utility. Modeling the household as a "black box," however, means that we have little other than the usual homogeneity restriction to guide us in the choice of a functional form for $m_0(\cdot)$. As with the welfare proxy approach reviewed above, the problem is not that one cannot estimate equivalence scales, but that one can estimate them in too many different ways, with results likely to differ with each specification.[11]

Household welfare as the subjective utility of the adults

In setting out the equivalence scale question in utility-theoretic terms (most notably in Muellbauer 1974), the equivalence scale question has come to be situated on a rather awkward conceptual base. The vocabulary and manner of formalization used is post-ordinalist revolution – "utility functions," "preferences," "compensation," etc. – but the interpretation given to "utility" is that of interpersonally comparable material welfare, more reminiscent of an earlier period in economics. It is not surprising that some economists have demanded that the equivalence scale literature be brought more up-to-date.

Pollak and Wales (1979) argued that a broader conception of "utility" vitiates the use of empirically estimated equivalence scales for welfare analysis. Household welfare, they argued, should be thought of as depending on household composition directly, as well as on commodity demands: "The expenditure level required to make a three-child family as well off as it would be with two children and $12,000, depends on how the family feels about children." An approach that ignores the direct effects of composition on household welfare is said to be merely "conditional," while true scales must depend on a more inclusive, "unconditional" welfare function. A similar criticism was raised by Franklin Fisher (1987: 522), and both articles have been favorably cited in other recent works.[12] Of course, since subjective utility is unobservable and not interpersonally comparable, "unconditional" equivalence scales are impossible to estimate. Richard Blundell and Arthur Lewbel (1991) have argued that, at best, demand information can tell us only how these "true" scales change with prices.

[11] The identification problem is further discussed in the published version of Nelson (1991), and Nelson (1993a).
[12] Pollak and Wales (or Fisher's) criticism has been favorably cited or adopted by Atkinson and Bourguignon (1989), Blundell and Lewbel (1991), Bourguignon (1989), Blackorby and Donaldson (1991), and Ray (1986), and has been further elaborated by Pollak (1991). It has also been discussed, less favorably, by Deaton and Muellbauer (1986) and Gronau (1988).

Other researchers have mentioned the endogeneity of household composition. When the equivalence scale question is phrased (as in Henderson 1950: 20) as regarding the relative "income which will compensate the parents for the material burdens of parenthood," the question naturally arises, "Why should they be compensated if parenthood is chosen?" Many economists are, in fact, quite willing to ignore the whole equivalence scale literature, either on the basis of disbelief in the basic assumption of interpersonal comparability of welfare levels, or on the basis that since adults generally choose to have children, the effect of children's presence on adult welfare must be as a net benefit rather than a cost.

This definition of equivalence scales differs from the early tradition and policy definition of equivalence scales both in definition of welfare (subjective utility vs. material well-being) and in the locus of welfare (parents vs. children). The subjective approach equates welfare with *happiness*. In contrast, most of the historical literature on equivalence scales, as well as the policy situations to which they are applied, are concerned with welfare in the sense of the *standard of living*. A cogent philosophical discussion of the distinction between "happiness" and the "standard of living" can be found in Sen (1987). The pleasure one (for example, a parent) may get from helping or being around someone else (for example, her child) may be part of a broad conception of welfare, or what Sen calls "well-being," but it is justly excluded from judgment of one's "standard of living" or well-being related to one's *own* life (ibid.: 28–9, examples added). A particular household member may certainly be made happier by the presence of other members, but (with limited resources) the additional demands on household resources also certainly reduce the member's ability (or "capability" in Sen's terms) to be, himself or herself, well-clothed, well-fed, well-rested, etc. Most distributional or policy studies center around questions of the distribution of economic means relative to needs in this latter sense, for example, the adjustment of poverty line income standards for family size. As questions of the distribution of pure subjective happiness are rarely raised in practical application, equivalence scales in the older, more materialistic, and more objective sense remain of great practical concern.[13]

---

[13] This is not a claim that, for example, a parent's happiness from having children is always irrelevant to public policy, only that such considerations are irrelevant to standard of living (and hence equivalence scale) comparisons. For example, policymakers may want to keep in mind the incentive effects on fertility, as well as standard of living consequences, when specifying how welfare or tax payments should change with household size. (The fact that child welfare and desired incentive effects may point to very different levels of grants or deductions, however, should encourage the use of multiple instruments: making children bear the brunt of their parent's decisions seems to be poor social investment policy.)

The criticism of equivalence scales on the basis that it makes no sense to "compensate" adults for choosing to have children, loses much of its strength if the locus of welfare concern is shifted to children. While children may or may not get direct enjoyment (or grief) from having siblings, it is quite clear that their material standard of living is compromised by too many siblings, and that they probably have rather little say in the decisions about family size. In fact, many of the critics of the adult-material-welfare view can be read as showing as much concern about its neglect of the material welfare of children as about the narrow definition of adult utility. Pollak and Wales (1979) close with a discussion of the need to investigate further "socially adequate consumption levels" for children, as opposed to adult preferences; Fisher's (1987) criticism of the use of adult material welfare focuses on the greater social utility of milk consumption in large families, than of whiskey consumption in small ones. In raising such concerns about children, the discussion harks back to the first definition of household welfare.

SUMMARY AND DIRECTIONS FOR FUTURE RESEARCH

The policy uses, and early history, of equivalence scales define "household welfare" in terms of a material standard of living, presumed to be shared by all household members. Scales that are based on estimates of physical "requirements," such as those underlying the current United States poverty line, are based on expert estimates of what household members could consume rather than on actual household behavior. Scales that use observed levels or shares of certain types of expenditure as welfare proxies avoid the prescriptive angle, but yield conflicting results. Over time, it has become more popular to express the equivalence scale question in modern choice-theoretic terms, but with the welfare level interpreted as the utility level of the adults. In the case of the Gorman–Barten model and of one foray into intertemporal modeling, the intra-household allocation is modeled as simply a byproduct of parental maximization of their own material welfare. These models may be perverse with respect to child welfare. In a reaction to this adult-material-welfare approach, it has been suggested that this is neglectful of the subjective utility that parents may receive from having children. As subjective utility is unobservable, the empirical estimation of "true" equivalence scales, it is said, reaches a dead end. However, the criticisms from this last direction only apply to the more recent interpretation of equivalence scales as related to adult preferences; seen in a broader historical and policy perspective, the question of equivalence scales has much to do with child (as well as adult) welfare.

At the present stage, it seems that there may be two main frontiers on which the equivalence scale literature could forge ahead. One would be to pursue the modern choice-theoretic approach consistently, that is, by focusing on adult subjective utility. This may be the most tractable using current theoretical tools, as it easily lends itself to discussion of, say, intertemporal maximization of utility, without posing difficult questions such as "whose utility?" or "defined over what?" While it may be the most rigorous and elegant way to proceed, intelligence would also have to be applied to finding new policy or empirical applications for the new developments. As a quite different question is asked, "motivating" the study or claiming its importance based on the traditional equivalence scale literature is inappropriate.

The other frontier would be to seek to improve the theory and empirical comparison of material standards of living across households of different composition, where the term "household" is understood to encompass all members. This is far messier, but also clearly has empirical and policy implications. The appropriate criteria for judging quality in this latter endeavor are not so much rigor and elegance, as reasonableness and usefulness. If two models are both based on implausible assumptions, there is no reason to believe that the greater elegance of one model makes it superior from a policy point of view.[14]

Given that no method appears to be clearly superior to all others, such policy-oriented research must continue with caution. In fact, the problem is even worse: the issues that need to be addressed will be in many cases broader than the traditional focus on simple expenditures allows. Two areas are sorely in need of further development: one, the definition of the standard of living, and two, the study of intra-family variation in the standard of living.

The concept of a standard of living can never be perfectly defined in a purely logical sense. As with many useful concepts, it is surrounded by a gray area. For example, the "material" standard of living is something of a misnomer if we consider access to education and other services as part of the definition. Yet in spite of the subject's resistance to absolutely definitive characterization, useful definitions may be possible for specific contexts and purposes. A middle ground in empirical work may be needed between the fine distinctions drawn by philosophers in the comparison of the standard of living of individuals (e.g. Sen's 1987 comparison of personal metabolic rates) and the very crude measures – total income or total consumption expenditures – used by most empirical researchers to make generalizations for the population. For example, the role of time in measurement of the standard of living has been neglected.

---

[14] Amartya Sen has written of the use of nutritional considerations as measures of poverty: "the recent tendency to dismiss the whole approach seems to be a robust example of misplaced sophistication" (1982: 14).

The Orshansky (poverty) scales, in assuming that all meals are prepared at home and that the household food buyer has the time and knowledge to shop wisely, and in using 1955 expenditure data (in which childcare expenses were presumably negligible), implicitly assume that one member of the household is a full-time homemaker. Works by Claire Vickery (1977) and Trudi Renwick and Barbara Bergmann (1993) are among the few to address the time use issue. Renwick and Bergmann use a "requirements" approach to defining a poverty line, within which necessary childcare and transportation expenditures are assumed to vary with the job status of the parent. Asset holdings represent potential consumption and a degree of security, and hence should not be completely ignored.[15] The quality and quantity of publicly provided goods, such as schools, roads, public transit, and parks (and, for comparisons between households in the U.S. and Europe, healthcare and daycare) may provide significant elements of the standard of living. Environmental factors, such as air quality, have clear standard of living implications that may vary with household composition (e.g. the presence of young children or the elderly). It is by no means easy to incorporate such factors as time use, assets, and extra-familial sources of welfare into measurement of equivalence scales. Though not every policy application would necessarily demand consideration of all of them, a narrow focus on familial income may be missing some of the major contributors to a family's standard of living.

Another area that needs investigation is possible intra-household variation in the standard of living.[16] While a presumption of equality may be a suitable working assumption in many cases, one cannot say anything about individual welfare until this point is explored. Research into this issue may be further advanced for developing countries (e.g. Haddad and Kanbur 1990; Sen 1984; Blumberg 1988) than for industrialized ones (e.g. Pahl 1989).[17] The question of intra-household variation has clear consequences for policy. For example, when aid to children is paid to their parent(s), a principle-agent problem is created. While the

---

[15] Some moves have been made to consider service flows from assets. The Census Bureau now includes, among its various measures of the distribution of U.S. income, one that attempts to take into account the net return on equity in owner occupied housing.

[16] I avoid stating this as the intra-household "distribution" or "allocation" of welfare, since these terms invite one to think in terms of dividing up a fixed pie. If there exist household economies of scale, such portioning out of household consumption or welfare is ill-defined.

[17] Lazear and Michael investigate the intra-household allocation of income in the U.S. (using Rothbarth Method assumptions), but "eschew making statements about welfare" (1988: 5). One interesting and suggestive result of Pahl's work is that questions regarding household finances, and the satisfaction of spouses with such arrangements, often receive conflicting responses depending on which member is interviewed: husbands are more likely than wives to report satisfaction and lack of conflict (Pahl 1989: 169).

public is concerned about children, it must (short of removing the child) act through the agent of the parent(s). Questions of how much welfare or publicly mandated child support, in cash or in kind, actually "gets through" to the children are little investigated, compared to their importance of this question in forming policy-makers' attitudes towards such programs. The question of whether it makes a difference to whom (mother or father) a payment is made has also been discussed in the context of some developing and industrialized countries (Blumberg 1988; Thomas 1990; Pahl 1989), but is little discussed, much less empirically investigated, in the U.S.A. Such questions require information bases distinct from the usual household consumption surveys, but perhaps it would be better to develop new empirical resources rather than to continue to search under the lamppost of standard consumption analysis.

In pursuing further research, it might be best to recover another aspect of early equivalence scale research that has also come to be overlooked: modesty about the applicability of results. Prais and Houthakker (1955), for example, limited their empirical work to the estimation of scales for specific food items. Sydenstricker and King's (1921) analysis was quite specifically applied to households within a given class, namely South Carolina mill workers. The search for one, true, definitive set of scales seems a chimera, since no completely superior method exists for their estimation. The pragmatic standard for policy guidelines, is, however, that scales be reasonable and well-informed; absolute truth and generality is not required. Further research may be much improved if, instead of pursuing the extremes of pure theoretical rigor on the one hand or pure ad hoc generation of a number (any number) on the other, a specific policy application is kept in mind and approached with flexibility and intelligence. Theory and policy need not be at odds, if they are made to address the same question.

7

FEMINIST THEORY AND THE INCOME TAX

EQUITY AND THE INCOME TAX

If you are married and a U.S. taxpayer, and you and your spouse both work, you may be paying more in U.S. income tax than you would without the marriage license. If you are single and working, and marry someone with no money income, your tax liability will go down. If you are a single parent with one dependent child, you may pay more in income tax than someone with the same income who has a nonworking spouse and no children. The differences can easily run in the thousands of dollars.

The current tax structure is the outcome of years of Congressional negotiations, and so is not entirely backed by explicit and consistent reasoning. The structure is, however, influenced by notions of "horizontal equity," or the belief that those in similar situations should be treated the same. The conception of horizontal equity not only requires that one answer the question of what "the same situation" means across units, but also, more fundamentally, that one determine a proper unit across which to make the comparison. The notion of horizontal equity requires a belief in a fundamental similarity among the units being compared, something that is much easier envisioned in the abstract, than in concrete cases. In fact, the translation of the ideal of horizontal equity into actual tax policy has been strongly influenced by patriarchal interpretations of what constitutes "the same situation" and what constitutes the "unit" of ethical concern. In this chapter, I argue that historical ways of viewing these questions have led to systematic inequities in the tax code, and discuss how feminist insights could transform the tax structure.

THE "PROPER UNIT" DISCUSSION

"Which is the proper unit of taxation, *the household* or *the individual*?" While discussion of the identity of the proper unit is of vital policy importance, there is something a little bit strange about the way this question is commonly formulated by economists and other commentators on public policy. The notion of "the household" as a unit supposes that households can be uniquely and discretely identified. If notions of the fairness of tax burdens "across households" are to be well defined, "households" must also have well-defined levels of well-being. The language of "the individual" as a unit, on the other hand, tends to focus attention on adult earners as the only tax-relevant human beings, with notions of dependency and other aspects of human relation pushed into the background.

Neither type of language seems adequate for the complexity of human relationships. Chapters 1, 2, and 3 discussed feminist insights into the separation/connection issues underlying notions of human identity. The "negative complementarity" so common to Western thinking – men as isolated, women as engulfed – is perhaps nowhere as obvious as in legal definitions of marriage.

Consider the legal definition of marriage historically embedded in English common law and carried over to the majority of states in the United States. According to William Blackstone writing in the late eighteenth century,

> By marriage, the husband and wife are one person in law: ... [The] very being or legal existence of the woman is suspended during marriage, or at least is incorporated ... into that of the husband, under whose wing, protection, and *cover* she performs everything ... [Her] condition during marriage is called her *coverture*.
>
> (quoted in Babcock *et al.* 1975: 562)

Or, as put by Justice Black in the U.S. in 1966, "This rule has worked out in reality to mean that though the husband and wife are one, the one is the husband." (Babcock *et al.*, 1975: 562) Common law neatly did away with the problem of a distinction between individuals and households. Single adult men were individuals. Married men were also individuals. Single women and married women disappeared into their fathers or husbands. Many modern statistical studies continue the common law presumptions in conceiving of the household as one "body," with a husband as its "head" and a wife and presumably children making up the lower organs. As noted in previous chapters, it is still common practice in many areas of applied economics to identify the preferences or characteristics of "the household" with those of the "head." This pattern of the treatment of women and children will be called "engulfment" (though terms such as "coverture," "subsuming," or even "dissolving" would also do).

This perception of the relationship between husband and wife-and-children affects not only how the household is perceived, but also how the larger world is perceived. With the wife-and-children absorbed in the household and its responsibilities of nurture and support, much of the men's activity takes place in the realms of politics and commerce. Legal and economic theory, based in a masculine realm of legally defined "individuals," can ignore the relationships that form the support systems for men's activity. The independent, autonomous "agent" of economic theory, for example, allows for theorizing free of questions of any relationship beyond that of the relationship of buyer and seller in exchange. But, with fairly rare and recent exceptions, the economic agent in most applied work is a household (or a business or some other aggregate of persons). How can this be made plausible? By engulfment again. Isolation and engulfment are ways of looking at the world that require each other: the creation of an isolated individual agent requires the engulfment in one "individual" (be it husband for a household, or owner for a firm) of a multitude of relationships among persons. When engulfment is complete, actual human relationships no longer complicate economic or legal theory or policy based on the supposedly independent individual as the unit of analysis.

Recall the analysis presented in earlier chapters, which argued that isolation and engulfment form the "negative complementarity" of the separation/connection dualism. The positive aspect of separation is the definition of individual identity; but taken too far, that is, unbalanced by a recognition of necessary social connections, the myth of the isolated, completely independent unit rears its head. The positive aspect of connection is the recognition of relationship to others; but taken too far, that is, unbalanced by a recognition of individuality, a person is engulfed (as in coverture) within the definition of another. The negative complementarity of isolation and engulfment should be replaced by the positive complementarity of individuation and relation. Persons are conceived of as *individuals in relation*.

The identification of "persons as individuals in relation" can be applied equally to both men and women. The idea that the identity of men and women is fundamentally the same, rather than fundamentally different, and that the identities of people of both sexes depend on both individuation and relation, has numerous consequences for policy discussions. First, it breaks down the "separate spheres" notion of sex "roles" that underlies so much of social, economic, and political discourse and practice. In particular, the notion that the "natural" sphere of action for a man is the public, economic and political realm, while the "natural" sphere of action for women is the private, familial realm, is rejected. In particular, the idea that childrearing is an exclusively female concern, rather than an activity that draws on the nurturing and stimulating skills of both parents, disappears with the recognition of, on the one hand, the mother's individuality, and, on the other, the father's responsibilities in relation. Biological differences between the sexes are not ignored, but are seen as minor in comparison to the similarities between men and women as humans. Second, understandings of other phenomena through the ideology of separate spheres, such as the classification of production within the household as "noneconomic," are also brought into question. If household labor does indeed significantly contribute to household economic welfare, then the application of standards of horizontal equity to the tax system should take this into account.

Third – and this is a more subtle but crucial point – the use of the language of unitary households on the one hand (representing engulfment) or autonomous individuals on the other (representing isolation) becomes immediately suspect. And how much of that language do we find in the history and proposals for reform of the U.S. income tax?

THE HISTORY OF THE U.S. INCOME TAX

In the original U.S. income tax law, enacted in 1913, the presumed taxpayer was referred to as a "citizen" or "person" (Marcuss and Nielsen 1985: 5). Exemptions were given for the first $3,000 of income for single "persons," and the first $4,000 of income for married "persons" (Pechman 1987: 313). No exemptions were allowed for children until 1917.[1]

Such an individualistic approach, however, soon became problematic because of differences in legal systems across states in the U.S.A. In the majority of states, marital property followed English common law in defining a man's earnings to be his own property. A married man with a homemaker wife would, in these states, file a return stating his full earned income and taking the married person exemption. A wife with no independent income would not file a return. Eight states, however, took their property laws from the civil laws of Spain and France. These declared that most income received by the spouses during marriage was "community property," in which each of the spouses had a legally defined interest (Babcock et al. 1975: 604). Supreme Court rulings allowed couples in these states to split their joint income evenly and file two separate federal returns, each using the lower marginal tax rates at the lower end of the tax schedule. Some common law states began enacting community property laws purely to gain this option for their residents. In 1948 it was decided to extend to all couples the tax treatment prevailing in the community property states: "income splitting" between marriage partners became the rule for all of the U.S.A. A new tax schedule for married couples filing jointly was devised, with

---

[1] For expositional simplicity, I will be concentrating on the treatment of earned income in this chapter, and will ignore the complications of property income.

brackets twice the width of those in the schedule for singles. While this change resulted in little or no savings for spouses with relatively equal earnings, for spouses with unequal earnings, like those with the traditional middle-class breadwinner–homemaker arrangement, the tax savings now extended in common law states could be substantial. The difference between the single and married filing jointly brackets were such that a single earner who married a low-earning or nonearning spouse could expect to receive a substantial "marriage benefit." Aside from the necessity of making changes to reduce geographical disparity, the income splitting arrangement has also frequently been justified as a better reflection of the ability to pay of the household, conceived of as an income-pooling unit. That is, one notion of fairness that can be found in the economic literature is that *households* with the same level of money income should pay the same taxes regardless of the actual distribution of earnings between the spouses.[2]

Since the "marriage benefit" did not extend to families that did not contain a married couple, the question arose as to the fair treatment of unmarried individuals with responsibility for the support of dependents. In 1952 yet another tax schedule was introduced, this time for these unmarried, dependent-supporting "heads of household." "Heads of household" were granted a rate schedule that provided one half of the benefit of joint filing, and a standard deduction between that of the single person and the married couple.

By 1969 it was considered unfair that single-person households should have to pay so much more than a married-couple household with the same income, and further changes were introduced. One rationale given for singles needing a break was that they did not benefit from the economies of scale in household living enjoyed by married couples. (Cohen 1983: 30) Singles were given a new, more generous rate schedule, designed to ensure payment of no more than about 20 percent more tax than an equal-income married couple who filed jointly. (Pechman and Engelhardt 1990: 11). Married couples who, because of relatively equal earnings, might find it advantageous to file separate returns at the new single rates were, however, precluded from doing so. The old, less generous rate schedule for singles was retained for married couples filing separate returns. (Marcuss and Nielsen 1985: 12) It was and still is rare that a couple would find it advantageous to use this schedule. Since 1969 there have existed four schedules, listed in decreasing order of generosity: married filing jointly, "head of household," single, and married filing separately. While the new breaks for singles did not erase the "marriage benefit" for spouses with very uneven earnings, spouses with earnings

---

[2] For example, Brazer (1980: 224) refers to the idea that the family is the appropriate taxable unit as "the traditional view".

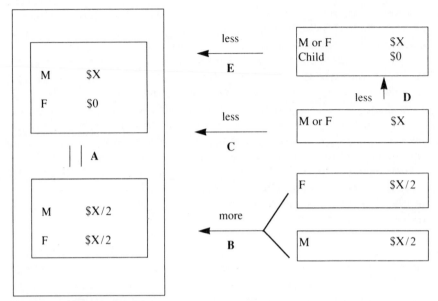

Figure 7.1 Schematic diagram of U.S. tax treatment[a]. Tax liabilities for households constructed of persons M,F, and Child, with earned incomes of $X or $X/2

Notes:

A Income splitting (codified since 1948)

B "Marriage tax" for two earners (due to benefits given to singles in 1969)

C "Marriage Benefit" for single earner marrying no-income spouse (due to income splitting)

D One half of benefit of income splitting (1952), plus an additional personal exemption

E One half of splitting is of less value than full income splitting

[a] This presentation makes many simplifications for exposition purposes, and is only intended to capture the general direction of the effects of U.S. income tax laws for earners in the middle-income ranges. The presentation assumes that each filter has only earned income, takes the standard deduction, does not qualify for any credits, and is not liable for minimum tax.

more equally split than about 75–25 now paid a "marriage tax" above what they would have paid as singles (Pechman 1987: 105)

A figure may make this structure clearer. Figure 7.1 compares the current treatment of equal-income households of various composition, assuming moderate levels of earnings and the simplest assumptions about filing (i.e., standard deductions, no minimum tax or tax credits). The large box on the left (and arrow A) illustrates how income splitting equalizes the tax burden of a household in which all the income is earned by one earner with the burden of an equal-income household in which each spouse earns one half of the total income. Two single earners would pay more if they married (the arrow B), while a single earner marrying a non-earner would see a lessening of the burden (the arrow C). A "head of household" with one dependent pays less tax than the single person with no dependent (the arrow D), but the married couple pays less than the "head of household" (the arrow E). As a concrete example, the 1993 tax liabilities for households with income of either $25,000 or $50,000 and under the simplest assumptions about filing, are given in the Appendix to this chapter. The chosen income levels are approximately one and two times (respectively) the earnings of an average U.S. production worker (determined by rounding off and inflating numbers used by Pechman and Engelhardt 1990).

The fact that single parents and two-earner couples with children may have childcare-related work expenses has not been entirely ignored in the tax law. Starting in 1954, such households were allowed a modest itemized deduction, in a similar fashion to treatment of other costs of employment. The deduction was expanded in 1971 and 1975, and in 1976 was changed to a tax credit, making it more available to low earning households (who rarely itemize deductions) (Ruttenberg and McCarthy 1984). Currently a single parent or two-earner couple can take a credit of 20 to 30 percent (depending on income) of childcare expenses up to $2,400 for one child, or up to $4,800 for two or more children. Taxpayers whose employers offer dependent care plans could choose, instead, to exclude from taxation up to $5,000 of income used to meet certain kinds of childcare expenses. If the "head of household" shown in Figure 7.1 has a young child and sufficiently high childcare expenses, for example, it is possible for the childcare tax credit or exclusion to narrow or even reverse in sign the gap between its payments and those of the married couple (see the Appendix, footnote c). Low income households with children may also be able to take advantage of the Earned Income Credit, lowering their tax liability or even turning it negative. In comparing the "head of household" to the married couples in Figure 7.1, however, it should be noted that the married couple has been assumed to be childless only to keep the size of the household constant for purposes of exposition. If a married couple has children, they may be able to take advantage of some of these childcare-related and child-related tax breaks in addition to benefiting from income splitting.

Congress also sought to ameliorate the burden on the two-earner couple in 1981, with the passage of a law allowing a deduction of 10 percent of the earnings of the spouse with the lower earnings, up to earnings of $30,000. Two reasons that were considered are given by Joseph Pechman (1987: 107). The first is the idea that "the one-earner couple has more ability to pay, because the spouse who stays at home produces income (in the form of household services) that is not subject to tax." The second is that "the high marginal tax rate on the earnings of the second spouse may discourage some from seeking employment." The problem of high marginal tax rates on secondary earners, usually considered to be the wives, has been discussed in the economics literature both in terms of intra-household equity and in terms of efficiency. (That is, the "optimal tax" literature and econometric estimates of women's labor supply elasticity combine to suggest high deadweight welfare losses from high marginal tax rates. For an example of this discussion, see Munnell 1980: 263–5.) The commitment of Congress to these ideas, however, was temporary: in 1987 the two-earner deduction was eliminated, "mainly for revenue reasons" (Pechman and Engelhardt 1990: 22).

THE CODE NEGLECTS HOUSEHOLD SERVICES

The point that most stands out about the U.S. tax code is the favorable treatment given to the one-earner couple. While the language of the tax code is sex neutral, it is obvious (from social mores and patterns of present differential earnings capabilities) that traditional couples in which the male is the breadwinner and the female a homemaker with no or low earnings, comprise the bulk of the beneficiaries. Consistent with separate spheres ideology, the dedication of the woman to home production is rewarded. Also consistent with separate spheres ideology, the value of that home production is not recognized as a source of imputable income (being part of the "feminine" realm, it is not "economic"). While unrenumerated work by women within the household was classified as a bona fide occupation in early nineteenth century British censuses, by the end of the nineteenth century this had changed. Housework came to be classified as "noneconomic," or "nonproductive" in both Britain and the U.S. (Folbre 1991). Women engaged in such work became classified by official statistics as "unoccupied," and were put with children, the ill, and elderly into the class of economic "dependents."

It is usually assumed that taxes should be based on ability to pay. As pointed out in the quote from Pechman above, if household services are counted as income (even in some very rough way) the ability to pay of an earner-and-homemaker couple with a given money income will be higher than that of a household in which earning the same money income requires that both adults work outside of the home. The two-earner couple has less time for leisure, and more need for money to pay for market goods to replace home production. Households with an earner and homemaking adult should also be compared, in terms of household services, to the household of an earner and a child. While older children may provide some household production, they almost certainly do not provide the same level of services as a full-time adult homemaker. Young children certainly provide less services, and in fact put extra demands on the adult earner. Why, then, with less household production should the single parent often have to pay more in taxes than the childless couple with the same money income?

While the source of the inequities of income splitting can be traced to community property law, the history of this law has some interesting wrinkles. Community property law has sometimes been regarded as more "pro woman" than common law. While the common law notion of coverture made the wife a dependent of the husband (at least until the Married Women's Property Acts of the mid- and late 1800s), community property at least in theory recognized the wife as a partner in marriage. As put by one U.S. judge, "Much may be said for the community property theory that the accumulations of property during marriage are as much the product of the activities of the wife as those of the titular breadwinner" (J. Douglas 1945, quoted in Williams 1978: 181). The adoption of community property principles may then be taken as recognition of the value of household production, at least when comparing contributions to the marriage between husbands and wives. The idea of valuing household production was not, however, extended outside the household, to the comparison of the ability to pay of households with and without a homemaker. Unfortunately for homemaking wives, their legal claim to half of the household income did not, through most of the history of community property states, mean that they actually gained economic power during the marriage. The power to manage the community property was still vested in the husband (Babcock *et al.* 1975: 604–13; Munnell 1980: 254).

One notion of equality notably absent from any discussion of the tax code is the equality of economic power within the household. The romantic language of chivalrous "protection" of the wife under coverture in common law, and the presumed "partnership" in owning (though not in managing) marital assets under the law of community property, give an illusion of beneficent treatment of wives while leaving decisions about their actual economic welfare firmly in the hands of their husbands. While many husbands no doubt have acted in ways that ensure a rough equality of material welfare, many other couples have no doubt found the arguments, "I earned it, so I get to choose how to spend it," influential in decision-making. Since the income-splitting approach discourages market labor and maintenance of job skills by the wife (conventionally seen as the "secondary" earner, due to social mores and generally lower earning prospects) by taxing her first dollar of earnings at the same marginal tax rate as the husband's last dollar of earnings, intra-household inequality is encouraged.

THE VOCABULARY OF "INDIVIDUAL OR HOUSEHOLD"

Throughout the history of the tax law, both before and after income splitting, one can see the struggles to define a discrete, independent, unit for tax purposes, to which notions of horizontal equity and ability to pay could be applied. Even the way of referring to the tax in the U.S. reflects this tendency to think of the world as made up of autonomous individuals: to distinguish the income tax applied to the household sector from the corporate income tax, it is usually referred to as the "individual" income tax, or the "personal" income tax, in spite of the relatively low proportion of people who file individually, instead of as part of some larger group.

As an extreme example of this bias towards "individual" treatment, in 1941 the Treasury proposed the restoration of geographical uniformity to the tax code by mandating joint filing and taxing the joint income of couples at the *individual* rate across both common law and community property states. (Marcuss and Nielsen 1985: 9) While the proposal was not enacted, it would have taken the doctrine that "the husband and wife are one, the one is the husband" to its logical conclusion. This treatment of the wife's income as the husband's for tax purposes was, in fact, part of the practice in England until 1994. (Pahl 1989: 162–5) The impact of a change in 1941 from the then-operative individual filing to such couple-as-individual taxation would have had little impact on single-earner couples in common law states: a change in exemptions at most. The impact on two-earner couples, who would no longer be allowed to file separate returns, would have been an instant halving of the width of the tax brackets, and a resultant increase in tax liability. More recently, Pechman has suggested such an application of the tax rate for singles to the married couple as a unit (Pechman 1987: 105; discussed in Munnell 1980: 250) as a way of avoiding single vs. married anomalies from income splitting, though he would also reinstate a special deduction for two-earner couples to lessen the unfairness to the two-earner couple.

In addition to suggestions for U.S. reform in the direction of consider-ing the couple as a single individual, there has been some recent discussion about changing to treating couples as two individuals, through a system of independent or "individual" taxation. There has been a historical trend, especially visible during the 1970s, towards such treatment in other industrialized nations (Munnell 1980: 275). France, (West) Germany, and the U.S. have been the notable holdouts (Pechman and Engelhardt 1990). An OECD publication states that this trend reflects "the desire to promote greater equality between the sexes, to encourage wives to take up employment and to protect the privacy of the individual." (quoted in Munnell 1980: 274). Reform of the U.S. tax system towards some form of individual taxation has been advocated by Harvey Brazer (1980), Alicia Munnell (1980) and June O'Neill (1983).

The notion of "individual" taxation covers, however, a wide variety of actual tax schemes. All governments that have moved to "independent" filing have seemed to find it desirable to incorporate some consideration of family and household relationships, through manipulation of exemptions, deductions, credits and rate schedules. (See Pechman and Engelhardt 1990.) While "individuals" may be the filers, the tax paid is usually not based on the individual's earnings alone, but also takes into account whether they are single or married, have children or are childless, and whether they are or are not the single earners in their household. The vocabulary of individualism, then, does not drive out consideration of family relationships. It does, perhaps, succeed in pushing them underground, to surface again in the form of adjustments that are ad hoc rather than integrated into the essential structure of the tax law.

There is a clear tendency in other U.S. policy decisions outside of the tax realm to identify the "individual" with the model of the isolated male. This is especially clear in labor issues, where the implicit assumption often seems to be that women can gain equal treatment with men only if they are willing to act in the ways in which males have traditionally acted. In particular, equal treatment seems often to require acting as if the presence of children had no impact on one's working life. The U.S.A. is far behind most other industrialized countries in such areas as parental leaves for childbirth or public support for childcare. Until the Family and Medical Leave Act of 1993, which requires employers to grant twelve weeks of unpaid leave to covered employees, there was no national parental leave policy. A substantial childcare bill was finally passed in 1990 that included funds for direct childcare assistance targeted towards lower income children, but only after years of struggle. Employed mothers in the U.S.A. are placed in a double bind: on the one hand, the workplace expects women to act like traditional men (who had wives at home to bear and take care of the kids), while on the other hand, childcare is considered to be primarily a woman's (as opposed to parental or social) responsibility. The recognition of the legitimate needs of the worker with family responsibilities, and the responsibility of men and society towards children, is very slow in coming.[3]

A second area in which the vocabulary of individualism causes what I see to be distortions of the issues is the idea that children are "consumption goods" to their parents. In this case, as was discussed in Chapter 6,

---

[3] An extreme example of the treatment of women in the mode of isolated individualism was the U.S. military's call-up policy for new mothers in the reserves during the war in the Persian Gulf. In early 1991 women were being called up to report for active service in the Gulf as little as ten days after childbirth, or face court martial (*The Sacramento Bee*, 2–6–91). Presumably the military is used to working with relatively relationship-free eighteen-year-old male draftees: "'At combat levels, we have always wanted young, single guys unencumbered with family concerns,' said Charles C. Moskos, a military sociologist at Northwestern University" (*The Sacramento Bee*, 2–9–91). Women and older parent reservists of either sex do not fit the bill.

only adults are granted individual agency, and children are reduced to nonhuman status. On this basis, it is sometimes suggested that tax exemptions for children have no justification. That is, parents' choice to spend some of their income on children is seen as no different from their decision to spend income on cars or refrigerators, and is therefore as little worthy of a tax benefit as any other consumption decision. (See, as an example of this argument, Brazer 1977.) While counter-arguments can be made supporting child exemptions on the basis of the social merit of the parents providing society with the next generation, or on the basis of the irreversibility of the childbearing decision, these arguments, both against and for exemptions, miss a major point by looking at children entirely as instruments for the furthering of parental or social welfare. What about the welfare of the children themselves? Because they do not live independently, does that mean they do not exist as humans under the tax law at all? A progressive tax structure with child exemptions leaves more income in the hands of the earners who provide for children's needs.[4] The setting of the size of exemptions might take into account incentive effects on parental fertility (with regard to societal pro- or anti-natal sentiments), but it should be remembered that children should not be penalized for fertility decisions in which they have no say.

A FRESH START

Rather than accept "the (presumably autonomous) individual" or "the (presumably unitary) family" as the proper unit of taxation, the feminist analysis outlined earlier suggests that one consider people to be individuals-in-relation. This suggests reevaluating the tax code in the light of two questions:

1 Which individuals should be required to pay taxes?
2 Which relationships, economic or otherwise, of these individuals should we consider to be important for tax purposes?

A full consideration of all the issues involved might take volumes of writing. Simplifying the questions by considering only earned income and assuming that the answer to (1) is, for most practical purposes, adult wage-earners, the rest of this section considers a few issues related to (2).

One issue is whether or not a marriage license should be relevant information for tax purposes. The current U.S. system takes it as a very important document, determining a variety of benefits and penalties. Harvey Brazer (1977: 239) supports reforms tending towards marriage

---

[4] Of course, while income in parental hands is necessary for child welfare, the coverture-like relationship of children to their parents means that it may not be sufficient. A discussion of the sensitive boundaries of responsibilities between parents and the state would take us too far afield from the present discussion.

neutrality in the tax code, on the rationale "that marriage or its dissolution through death or divorce, cohabitation of a sustained or sometime sort, or what have you, are simply not the concern of the Internal Revenue Code." The rising number of couples cohabiting without marriage (and the small but growing number of two-household "commuter marriages") certainly puts into doubt any naive assumption about the necessity (or sufficiency) of marriage for household formation.

A second issue is that of household economies of scale. My own research (Nelson 1988) as well as that of others suggests that people who combine into households may need significantly less resources than people living alone, to reach the same level of economic welfare. Some may argue, then, that rather than focusing taxation on the earner-plus-dependents, one should look for the unit over which intra-household public goods like housing are shared. A single person living alone, by this reasoning, should bear less taxes than the single person cohabiting or in a group house (as well as less than a person in a married-couple household), since she or he has higher "expenses." I believe, however, that economies of scale should probably be irrelevant for taxation for the same reason as given above for a preference for marital neutrality: how people choose to live is their own business. To the extent that in the long run people can sort themselves into their preferred living arrangements, it should be irrelevant to the government whether people decide to buy privacy by living in small units, or forgo privacy in favor of some other consumption goods by seeking economies of scale.

A third issue is that of presumed income pooling within households. As pointed out above, the idea that households with equal income should pay equal taxes, regardless of the distribution of earnings between the spouses, relies on the idea that the consumption level of individuals within a household is purely a function of aggregate income. Obviously this relies on a strong assumption about intra-family distribution. Perhaps, since it is hard for policy-makers to see the inside workings of households, it would be better to enact policies that are likely to encourage intra-household equality, rather than to presume intra-household equality and continue policies that may promote unequal earning and unequal power between household members.

A fourth, and very important issue, concerns relationships of economic dependency. Obligations to support persons unable to support themselves (the very young, very old, or disabled), whether legal or voluntary, and whether within or across households, should be taken into account in the tax structure. I have already commented on child exemptions above. Note, however, that if the criteria for classification as a dependent revolves around lack of ability for self-support, homemaking spouses (or any able-bodied, prime age adult) would not qualify. This would be a change from current U.S. law, in which the married couple who files jointly claims two exemptions even if only one spouse works outside the home (and receives a higher standard deduction than a single person), and in which one cohabiting partner can claim the other as a dependent if they meet qualifications for support, and live in a state where cohabitation is legal (O'Neill 1983: 12). Such a view may also change the way in which support given across the boundaries of "nuclear" families is counted. As Pechman (1987: 105) points out, the current "makeshift arrangement does not deal with the problem satisfactorily. For example, single taxpayers who support aunts or uncles in different households receive no income-splitting benefit; if they support an aged mother, they receive these benefits." While benefits may be conferred by exemptions rather than income splitting, recognition of more situations of economic dependency could break down the arbitrariness of the current boundaries. Such extended tax benefits could be especially beneficial for some minority and immigrant groups in the United States, whose networks of economic support stretch far beyond the "nuclear" family bounds.

A MODEST PROPOSAL

The most natural implementation of the idea of "persons in relation," in regards to the tax code might be the definition of a unit of taxation as an individual earner plus his or her dependents. By "dependents" I mean those persons who, unable to support themselves for reasons such as youth, advanced old age, or chronic disability, rely on the earner for their economic support. Able-bodied adults are never engulfed, in this definition: even if they are nonearners, their productive capacity is recognized and they are never considered as dependents. This definition of the unit of taxation is not a simple definition by relation, as the individual's earnings are considered separately from the earnings of other household members. The unit is in general smaller than a household. Neither is it a simple definition by individuality, since economic relationships are explicit in the definition from the outset (rather than grafted on ad hoc). The unit is in general larger than the individual.

The simplest way to see the results of this structure is by looking at Figure 7.2. Assume, for simplicity, that the tax code involves only subtraction of personal exemptions (one for each earner, plus one for each dependent), with the remaining income taxed according to a progressive rate structure. The single adult who has a child may claim two exemptions in filing taxes on his or her earnings: one for him or herself and one for the child. Otherwise, all earners shown in this figure file taxes on only their own earnings, claiming only their own (nontransferable) personal exemption. The nonearning adult neither files nor provides anyone with an exemption.

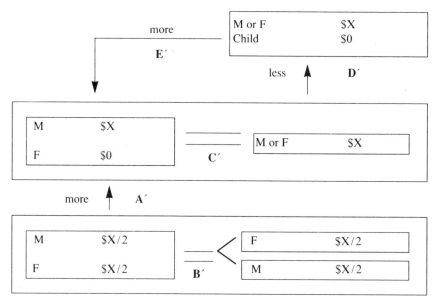

Figure 7.2 Taxation based on earner plus dependents. Tax liabilities for households constructed of persons M,F, and Child, with earned incomes of $X or $X/2

Notes:
A′ Larger tax burden on household with greater household production
B′ Marriage neutrality (two filings, each with one exemption)
C′ Marriage neutrality (one filing, one exemption)
D′ Additional personal exemption for child
E′ Child, but not nonearning spouse, merits exemption

The most striking fact about this structure is its complete marriage neutrality: in neither the case of the two earners who marry, nor in the case of the single earner that marries a nonearning spouse, is tax liability changed by marriage.

The second notable difference from the present structure is the lessened tax burden of the two-earner couple *vis à vis* the one-earner couple. Even if the tax code were proportional, the two-earner couple's taxes would be lower since they each claim a personal exemption, while the one-earner couple has only one personal exemption. Progressivity of the rates would increase this difference in burdens. While obviously not a perfect way of taxing the household production of the homemaker spouse, disallowing an exemption for an able-bodied spouse yields some of this effect while avoiding a controversial imputation of an actual dollar value for such labor. The work disincentives for "secondary" earners would disappear ("primary" or "secondary" being meaningless terms under independent filing), with likely salutary

111

effects on the actual intra-household equality of economic power.

Some might object to the first dollar of earnings of the spouse of a rich person being exempted (by the activation of that person's own personal exemption) or taxed at a low rate, on grounds of vertical equity. (See, for example, Minarik 1983, who phrases it as a case of a woman "leaving home" to work for *Ladies Home Journal*.) It is true that, taking the household as the income unit, a household with a very high single-earner income could yet increase its income over some range "tax-free" through market entry by a nonworking spouse. Lower income single persons or two-earner couples have no such tax-free margin. However, this scenario is not much different than that under the current system, when the rich person and new worker are cohabiting instead of married.

As seen in Figure 7.2, the single parent would pay less than the single person without dependents, just as was the case in Figure 7.1. Under this proposal, however, the single parent would also unambiguously have a lower tax burden than the one-earner couple with the same income, as is sensible when one takes into account household production. The size of these tax differentials would depend on the value of the extra personal exemption this household claims because of the presence of the (true economic) dependent. Since the individual-and-dependents approach does not provide the benefits from partial income splitting given in the current code, some adjustment of the value of the exemption for children might be necessary if the dollar value of the single person vs. "head of household" differential were to be maintained. As women comprise the vast majority of single parents in the United States, many of whom are low income, changes affecting this filing status are particularly of interest to feminists.

ONE MODIFICATION

In one important way, the simple rule of earner-plus-dependents, and the definition of dependents I gave above, would need modification in the current U.S. situation. One needs to take into account that children are not only dependent on adults for financial support, but also, at very young ages, are dependent on intensive physical and emotional caregiving. As I discussed above, the U.S.A. lags far behind many other countries in supporting working parents in caring for their children. The denial of exemptions to adults who stay at home to look after very young children, given the lack of other social changes and programs, may seem to many to be too harsh. Tax code modifications are a possible means of supporting childbearing, infant–parent bonding, and early child development – if done carefully.

Reinstating the personal exemption (much less income splitting) for all nonearning spouses would, of course, be a badly targeted policy since many homemakers have no young children. Present tax-related policies tend to be a hodgepodge, subsidizing either paid childcare or a parent staying at home with an infant, but not a mixture. On the one hand, the current Childcare Tax Credit only benefits parents of infants if they put the child into paid care. On the other hand, California in 1990 instated a new state tax credit of up to $1,000 for a parent of an infant provided he or she stays home with the child for the child's first year of life (Chapter 1347, Sec. 2 of the 1990 Reg. Session). Beginning in 1991, low income working families have been able to take an extra federal Earned Income Credit for children born during the tax year – but only if the childcare exclusion or credit is not claimed. While many advocates believe that the next step after getting twelve weeks of unpaid leave into Federal law is to push for extending the period of the leave and making it paid (along the European pattern), such policies are controversial even among feminists. Extended paid leaves, especially if offered to or taken up primarily by mothers rather than fathers, are seen by some as subtly enforcing the domesticity of women.

Rather than subsidizing either one form of care or the other, a tax policy that would be more neutral with respect to the parents' early work and childcare arrangements might be to give an extra tax exemption (or credit) to parents for the year of a child's birth. Parents could use the tax savings to subsidize relatively expensive infant childcare, or to reduce work hours (allowing the tax savings to subsidize a period of unpaid leave), or to subsidize some combination of the two forms of care, depending on their own needs, skills, resources, and the needs of their particular child.[5] Extension of the duration of unpaid leave, and allowing it to be used more flexibly (e.g. for part-time work, perhaps by both parents in a two-parent household) would increase the potential welfare gains from the tax benefit.[6] Such legislation combining an extra tax exemption (or credit) with mandated offers of unpaid parental leave might be more politically palatable than either extra childcare subsidies or extended paid leaves. If one compares such a policy to, for example, a policy of employer-paid leaves at a given percentage of the employee's usual earnings, additional advantages emerge as well. The unpaid-leave-plus-exemption (or credit) approach would concentrate more benefits on low-earning workers, and diffuse some of the burden on employers.

[5] Such a policy should be seen as complementary to, rather than competitive with, a program of widespread childcare assistance for children of any age. The issue at hand concerns provision for infants, for whom care must be particularly intensive.

[6] Allocating the period of unpaid leave between parents on a "use-it-or-lose it" basis could also help to promote equity between men and women in the household. For example, the parents could be entitled to six months' leave each, giving them a year of leave if they both use it, but only six months if one refuses to take time off.

APPLICATIONS

RESISTANCE TO REFORM

As criticism from feminists regarding the tax code has already been heard, and proposals for some sort of independent filing have already been floated (O'Neill, Munnell, Brazer), it is interesting to note the responses of the critics of reform.

One reason for the bias of the tax code towards the traditional, one-earner married couple is no doubt an ideological one. It is no secret that many current U.S. political conservatives and religious fundamentalists believe that the maintenance of civilization depends on the maintenance of the traditional, patriarchal household. Certainly this could have been the viewpoint of many of the legislators who have participated in the passage of various tax acts.

While to many observers such ideas may seem old fashioned, they have insinuated themselves into current, professional discourse as well. Joseph Stiglitz, for example, in his widely used 1988 textbook for undergraduate public economics states, "A tax system that encourages women to enter the labor force may have adverse effects on family structure, and, in particular, on the educational attainments of children" (1988: 529) He includes supporting references to carefully selected well-known (male) authorities. One may well ask, "'Adverse' by whose criteria?" Continuance of a patriarchal structure is certainly not in everyone's interest. And, while controversies in education are still being fought, one may ask, "What is the effect on a girl's educational ambition and attainment if she knows that wife and mother is the only career open to her?" The phrasing of options in such a way as to pit women's interests against those of their children is a technique of resistance to feminist reform that seems particularly underhanded.

The commentaries by Joseph Minarik (1983) and Edwin Cohen (1983) on O'Neill's (1983) individual taxation proposal are also particularly interesting in the ways they try to maneuver around feminist criticism. In addition to appealing to notions of "the basic institution of marriage" (Minarik 1983: 25) and the "well-functioning marriage" in which "it is immaterial whose income it is and who pays the expenses" (Cohen 1983: 29), resistance to O'Neill's suggestion takes two other forms. Cohen trivializes the question of the value of household labor, comparing the nonmarket production of a nonearning spouse to his own benefit from playing tennis (p. 29). Minarik (p. 27) (and, implicitly, Cohen: 31) trumpets the fact that the tax code is now sex-neutral in language, and concludes that this makes it nonsexist in application – ignoring centuries of legal and social influence on how the breadwinner and homemaker roles come to be assigned (p. 27).

Lastly, there are administrative and legal arguments against individual taxation, such as the difficulties presented by the distinction between

114

common law and community property states. While certainly these need addressing, Munnell (1980) points out that numerous other jurisdictions have made individual taxation workable, and that legal precedent exists in the U.S.A. for overriding some of the states' community property laws.

DIRECTIONS FOR RESEARCH

If nothing else, the feminist analysis of separation and connection teaches us to be wary of the extremes of isolation and engulfment. If a proposal is couched in language of pure individualism: be suspicious. If a proposal assumes the engulfment of a number of individuals into an easily manipulable (i.e., manipulable "as if" an individual) unit: be suspicious.

I have argued in this chapter that the U.S. tax code, which currently in ideology and in practice promotes male individualism and female subservience to relationships, should be reformed in the direction of a structure based on the idea of persons-in-relation. The structure I suggest is highly simplified, and as yet leaves many questions, such as those pertaining to the treatment of property income, how child exemptions would be allocated between parents, or the questions of social security taxes and benefits, unanswered. I hope that future policy research in the U.S. will address these questions, and learn from the experience of researchers and policy-makers in countries that already have some form of individual-plus-dependents taxation.

What is most striking, though, about U.S. discussion of "the proper unit of taxation" is not so much the fact that it takes into account too few options. The most striking fact is the infrequency with which the issue is discussed at all, among academic economists. Public finance economists, as other economists, tend to find it much more fun and rewarding to work out the theoretical details of models involving hypothetical autonomous, rational "agents." The more abstract and mathematical the model, the better. The question of whether the insights gained about the behavior of the "agent" within the context of the model can be transferred to yield insights about anyone or any group in the actual economy is asked much more rarely than it should be. But such a gendered priority put on isolation has been discussed in other chapters.

APPENDIX

1993 Tax Code applied to households described in Figure 7.1 assuming Adjusted Gross Income of X = $50,000 or X/2 = $25,000. Standard Deduction, no tax credits[a]

Tax liabilities

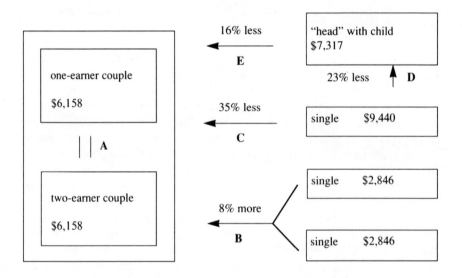

Tax calculations:

	Single $	Single $	Married, joint[b] $	"Head of household"[c] $
Adjusted Gross Income	25,000	50,000	50,000	50,000
(less) Standard Deduction	3,700	3,700	6,200	5,450
(less) Personal Exemptions: Number times $2,350	1	1	2	2
(yields) taxable income	18,950	43,950	39,100	39,850
(by tax table) tax owed	2,846	9,440	6,158	7,317

Notes:
[a] *Source*: United States Department of the Treasury 1993.
[b] Separate filing by the two-earner couple would save them $8 in taxes.
[c] If this household has childcare expenses of at least $2,400 for a child under age 13, it may qualify for a tax credit of 0.20 × $2,400, reducing its tax liability to $6,837. In this case, the married couple pays only 10 percent (rather than 16 percent) less. If this earner's employer offers a dependent care plan, the earner may instead choose to exclude up to $5,000 spent on childcare from his or her Adjusted Gross Income, reducing taxable income to $34,850 and the tax liability to $5,917. In this case, the married couple would pay 4 percent *more* taxes. If this household were to be compared to a childless couple household at a substantially lower income level, the Earned Income Credit could cause this household to pay substantially less than the childless couple or even get a payment from the government. In 1993 the earnings cutoff for qualifying for the Earned Income Tax Credit for this household would have been $23,050. Since the value of the tax credit is very small close to this cutoff, the reversal of the relative tax liabilities of a childless couple and "head" with child tax liabilities (in the absence of other exclusions and credits) would occur below this income amount.

8

FEMINIST ECONOMICS, EMPIRICAL ECONOMICS, AND MACROECONOMICS

NOT JUST A FAMILY MATTER

Most of the applications of feminist economics in the preceding chapters have focused, in one way or another, on family issues. This is perhaps not surprising, since making family issues visible has been an important part of the feminist agenda. The one application that has not focused on families (Chapter 4) has been in an area considered by most economists to be outside of the core of the discipline (i.e., the history of economics). But what does feminist economics have to say about other areas of economics considered more central, beyond the general criticism of narrow micro-models voiced earlier?

Sometimes the question is asked, "Where would a feminist economics give us a different result, in macroeconomics, or industrial organization, or finance, or any other field?" By now it should be clear that feminist economics does not change the results of investigation by prescribing them directly, but instead influences what we would take to be satisfying results by changing the criteria by which we judge research to be reliable and interesting. Economics is sorely in need of a new system of values, if it is to be able to generate more reliable, more scientific and objective (in the "strong" sense) knowledge. In this chapter, I shall present specific examples of how a less masculine-biased view of what economics is about would change the character of two (overlapping) areas: macroeconomics and empirical economics.

MACROECONOMICS

The GDP issue

One feminist critique relevant to macroeconomics is fairly well known. The exclusion of unpaid work at home, work that historically has been largely done by women, from calculations of Gross Domestic Product (GDP) serves to help make such work invisible. Nearly all feminists would agree that work at home is actually work, rather than "leisure," and that it is actually production in the same sense of many other items already included in GDP. The inclusion of monetary calculations of the value of this work in GDP measures is, however, not a major issue for many feminists, and is even opposed by some. On the one side are writers such as Marilyn Waring (1988) who argue that until household unpaid labor is included directly in the GDP statistic, women's unpaid work will go unvalued and neglected, with myriad and serious policy consequences. On the other side, Barbara Bergmann (1994) argues that emphasizing the value of housework may be done with the aim of glorifying the housewife role, to the detriment of women's drive for equality. In the middle are feminists who would like to see unpaid work become visible as real production, and become more adequately studied, but who are less directly focused on the issue of GDP statistics. The serious study of household production is seen, in this middle position, as necessary so that time spent by parents in caring for children is recognized as a contribution to national human capital, so that the division of household labor can be studied, so that macroeconomic development policies are well targeted, and so that macroeconomic stabilization policies will be less likely to rely on absorption of costs by the unaccounted-for household sector (e.g. Bened́a 1992, Bakker 1994, Folbre 1994). Whether the particular GDP figure is revised is seen as less important.

Regarding macroeconomics, the main implication of the GDP critique is that GDP series are inaccurate as measures of production. In particular, while women have increasingly entered the labor force and had their market wages counted in GDP, one would expect that home production has experienced some corresponding decrease. GDP growth is upward biased to the extent that this decrease is not noted. Yet this is just another problem among myriad with GDP. I have no doubt that there was sexist bias involved in dismissing household labor when constructing the system of national accounts, since though the creators otherwise went to great lengths to figure out how to include the value of such other hard-to-account-for, unmarketed, items such as the services of owner-occupied housing or government production. Home production has been considered, sometimes just as "women's work," but even more often as *non*work, by economists and census takers (Folbre 1991).

But I also think that the major policy-related problem lies, not so much with underaccounting for household production in GDP, but in taking GDP numbers too seriously as a measure of welfare. GDP is an admittedly crude measure of market and government economic activity, and I see no reason that it could not be kept around for that limited purpose. Measurement of welfare, on the other hand, is fundamentally multidimensional. Not only should one include nonmarketed as well as marketed production, but one should distinguish welfare-enhancing from welfare-reducing (e.g., polluting) production, account for distribution across the population (not just across households, since households also have internal distributions), and account for the sustainability of production by looking at what is happening to the resource base. Outcome measures, such as statistics on educational achievement, morbidity, literacy, infant mortality, unemployment, exposure to crime, air quality, etc. can also be helpful in describing the standards of living achieved by a nation's residents (see, e.g., United Nations Development Program 1990; Nussbaum and Sen 1993). I see a key role of the feminist critique to be in questioning the methodological reductionism of (in spite of the weak "we know its not a welfare measure" paragraph in the introduction to every macroeconomics textbook) focusing so much attention on a single number, rather than in the improvement of this single number.

Feminism and the New Classical Macroeconomics

The feminist methodological critique has other implications as well. As a regular teacher of undergraduate macroeconomics, but not an active researcher in the area, I take a view of new developments in the field that is somewhat from the sidelines. From this perspective, at least, the most dramatic change in macroeconomics in the last decade and a half has been the rising influence of New Classical Economics, associated with the work of Robert Lucas, Edward Prescott, Thomas Sargeant, and others. This group of economists has also been sometimes loosely (and rather inaccurately) referred to as the Rational Expectations or Real Business Cycle school. The fundamental assumption that sets this group apart from other macroeconomists is the assumption of continuous market clearing, (i.e. that all agents are able to optimize successfully). By taking models of individual optimization as the starting-point for macroeconomic theorizing, New Classical economists function within a constricted methodological program. Lucas, for example, claims that the assumptions of rational choice modeling provide the "only 'engine of truth' that we have in economics" (Lucas 1987: 108). Such economists tend to condemn any variation away from dynamic microeconomic market-clearing models of their own particular flavor as ad hocery of the most despicable sort. Economics progresses by developing theories from first principles, it is said, parts of which can then (according to some of New Classicals) be formally tested using sophisticated econometric techniques. Only research programs that fit within these molds are judged to be real economics.

The effect of this school on macroeconomics has been enormous. The undesirability of unemployment, for example, an assumption that was previously at the core of macroeconomics, is questioned. Unemployment is redefined as just one more optimizing choice by a rational agent: "To explain why people allocate time to a particular *activity* – like unemployment – we need to know why they prefer it to *all* other available activities" (Lucas 1987: 54; emphasis in original). The main answer to "why they prefer it" given by Real Business Cycle theorists is that the unemployed are "intertemporally substituting leisure," i.e., taking a vacation. While when it is expressed in bare English most observers would find this theory ludicrous, no macroeconomics textbook that wants a mainstream market can, at the time of this writing, fail to have at least one chapter that works out this theory in mathematical and graphical detail. Some recent popular textbooks (e.g., Abel and Bernanke 1992) take Walrasian market clearing as the default assumption throughout.

The inroads of the New Classical school have not gone unchallenged. One tactic of defense in the New Keynesian school is to fight the New Classicals on their own ground, by, for example, building up explanations for involuntary unemployment from the same micro-foundations, or by criticizing the New Classicals for their own lapses from absolute rigor. Many economists would argue that some good work has come out of this.

But the feminist critique of the standards of value in current economic methodology can join forces with another form of resistance to the New Classicals, expressed vociferously by such macroeconomists as Alan Blinder (1989) and Thomas Mayer (1993). This critique questions not just the New Classical conclusions, but the whole New Classical methodological program. Only if one accepts that economies are essentially abstract Walrasian auctions; that all theory must be conform to the formal dictates of such a model; and that all empirical knowledge about the economy must come via formal tests of hypotheses rigorously derived from such a model, does the New Classical theory score a coup. To put it in gender-oriented terms, it is only if one believes that the culturally "masculine" notions of rational individual choice and rigorous formal analysis are definitive of science, that one has to play on the New Classical playground. The feminist analysis of this book, in arguing that emotions and institutions, and rich metaphorical analysis and concrete observation, are equally valid in defining quality economic practice, should help steer macroeconomics back to a more useful path.[1]

---

[1] See also Bergmann (1987) for another discussion of New Classical economics by a feminist economist.

Feminist macroeconomics?

One can already point to two areas in which a feminist analysis extends or complements such a richer macroeconomic practice. While most macroeconomists consider agent expectations about the economy in only a purely formal and statistical manner, Lee Levin presents a theory of investment that takes into account the feminist insight that knowledge is socially and emotionally constituted. In viewing investors' expectations as "the unstable product of convention" (1993: 13), Levin provides justification for Keynes' notion of "animal spirits." Instead of borrowing only from statistics to model expectations, Levin borrows from sociological and psychological studies of rumor, evaluation of belief, fad and fashion, cognitive dissonance, and contagion theory. All of the latter, of course, sound "soft" to the economist trained to believe that rigor is defined by mathematics. But I believe it will be shown that Levin's approach will be the more adequate one for gaining insight into investor behavior.

Feminists and macroeconomists can also enter into dialogue about labor markets. A theme reiterated by many macroeconomists critical of New Classical theory, and especially by George Akerlof and Janet Yellen (1988, 1990), Robert Solow (1990), and Alan Blinder (1989), is that one factor keeping actual labor markets from closely resembling the supply-and-demand graphs of microeconomic theory is the importance of perceived fairness in wage-setting relationships. Work has been done showing that perceived fairness plays an important role in price setting as well (Kahneman *et al.* 1986). Some of this idea is incorporated in New Keynesian "efficiency wage" theory, though sometimes (rather contrived) attempts are made to formulate the dependence of workers' effort on wage in purely efficiency terms without any reference to issues of perceived equity.[2] While not explicitly feminist, the work on fairness clearly challenges the profession's preference for efficiency arguments to the exclusion of equity explanations – a preference that has been argued to be an outgrowth of gender bias (see Chapter 2).

None of the macroeconomist authors in this area, however, have apparently recognized a complementarity between this recognition of "the labor market as a social institution" (Solow 1990) and the arguments of many feminists about comparable worth (e.g., England 1992). Many feminists argue that the types of jobs held by women are systematically paid less than their worth to the employer. Most economists dismiss this argument, referring to arguments that competitive markets will drive

---

[2] Mankiw (1994: 130–31), for example, mentions health, turnover, adverse selection, and moral hazard as justifications for efficiency wages, but never fairness. Abel and Bernanke (1992: 449), on the other hand, do briefly mention fairness as an issue. Their emphasis, however, is on squeezing the problem into a standard-looking graphical analysis, rather than in exploring the richer model of human motivation.

women to be paid their marginal product. But what if Akerlof, Yellen, Solow and Blinder are right, and perceptions of fairness support many actual, non-market-clearing wage systems? And what if it has been socially perceived that "feminine" activities are of little worth, so that therefore it is only "fair" to pay them less? Once one has opened the door to considering social influences on economic outcomes, one can hardly dismiss the possibility of social gender biases out of hand. Turning the argument around the other way, one might consider that the New Classical advantage in avoiding such subjects may be part of its appeal, at least to those who derive practical benefits from current notions of fairness and legitimacy.

Empirical macro

Thomas Mayer (1993: 132) has referred to the common practice in macroeconomics of setting high standards of rigor for the development of theory, but much looser standards for empirical testing, as "driving a Mercedes down a cow-track." It is an example, he writes, of judging programs by "the principle of the strongest link" (i.e., rigor in formal theorizing) instead of, more validly, judging by the strength of the weakest link. Lawrence Summers (1991, 146) has referred to use in macroeconomics of theory-driven, formal econometric testing to the exclusion of more pragmatic, informal empirical work as an approach that "virtually always fails." While both Mayer's and Summers' criticisms concentrate on macroeconomics (Keynesian as well as New Classical), their criticisms are equally valid for other fields as well.

EMPIRICAL ECONOMICS

The state of the art

Mayer and/or Summers criticize economists for (variously) data mining (i.e., continuing to refine one's statistical specification until the results fit one's theory); overemphasizing and/or misusing standard significance tests; confusing statistical significance with substantive significance; failing to do adequate sensitivity tests; failing to put any importance on doing replications; overusing readily available data sources; neglecting to extend study to alternative data sources; selectively reporting results; failing to pay heed to issues of data quality; and hiding implausible explanations of causal relations behind obscuring walls of mathematical formalism. No wonder Mayer suggests that ("at least in some cases") formal testing might be regarded as merely "ceremonial" (1993: 148), or Summers that it represents only a "scientific illusion" (1991). Criticisms of economists' ill-founded pretension to precision have also been expressed by Edward Leamer (1983), Donald McCloskey (1985), and Barbara Bergmann (1987).

All of these writers claim that economics would be improved by increased attention to neglected areas of empirical work (such as data compilation), along with a complementary humility concerning the supposed "rigor" of econometric results. Summers suggests that it is informal, pragmatic empirical work, characterized by "verbal characterizations of how causal relations might operate rather than explicit mathematical models" (1991: 130), and by a search for stylized facts rather than formal evaluation of precise hypotheses, that has actually been successful in influencing our beliefs about the economy.

One might ask if empirical economics in general is really in such bad shape. As a practicing empirical economist – and hence both a regular writer and reader of empirical articles, published and unpublished – I would answer in the affirmative. I have been particularly concerned with the lack of attention to the gathering of data, to the quality of the data used and to the mechanics of its handling. For a discipline that considers itself "scientific" relative to the other social sciences, the lack of consideration for basic empirical technique is appalling. In the physical and biological sciences graduate students are required to do laboratory work and keep lab books. In most of the other social sciences graduate students spend some time in a "research methods" course that includes issues such as survey design, and often gain experience in actual fieldwork as well. Economics graduate students, however, usually receive no training in skills of observation or survey techniques, nor even in techniques for responsibly cleaning, describing, and documenting work with data garnered secondhand. While they may use data in exercises for econometrics classes, these classes usually emphasize statistical theory to the near exclusion of issues of data and functional form. Standards of data use put on theses and dissertations are usually not much higher, and primary data-gathering for a dissertation is rare and little rewarded. That some economists do end up doing empirical work to reasonable standards is due more to an informal apprenticeship system and on-the-job (re)training than to economics education.

Replication of studies, standard procedure in many natural sciences, is almost nonexistent in economics. The National Science Foundation funded a study of replication in economics, in which researchers asked authors of articles published in the *Journal of Money, Credit and Banking* in the previous two years to provide them with the data they used. They found that, "Approximately one-third of the authors (20) never replied to our repeated requests, and an additional one-third (20) replied that they could not furnish their programs or data ... Fourteen wrote that they had lost or discarded their data" (Dewald *et al.* 1986). Of the data submitted, most were considered to be inadequately documented.

The National Science Foundation also has a policy that its grantees in economics should place their data in archives and footnote their availability. Compliance with this requirement, according to an NSF staff member, has been "miserable" (Newlon 1992).

Value judgments attached to "hard" versus "soft" data also deserve reexamination. Economists' skepticism about asking people about the motives behind their behavior is so strong that Alan Blinder (1991) devoted a full section in a recent piece on price stickiness simply to justifying the use of such interview survey data. While judged by a standard of Cartesian "proof," such evidence may be inadmissible, judged by a standard of broader and more practical learning about economic functioning such data can be seen as potentially contributing important information. A recent conference of the International Association for Feminist Economics included presentations by a historian and a sociologist on the techniques of doing oral history studies. Economists who overcome their prejudice in this area may be surprised at the sophistication in technique and the attention given to issues of validity and replicability demonstrated by those highly skilled in such "soft" and qualitative methods. As was argued in Chapter 3, personal experience should also not be discounted among ways in which we – consciously or not – gather data. One part of the practice of striving for objectivity should be an examination of how the things that one believes from one's own experience may influence one's research.

Such a neglect of the practical requirements of serious empirical work reflects a romance with abstraction, formalization, detachment and precision. Such a neglect of the concrete, verbal, connected and approximate in methods of research is, I have argued in other chapters, connected to perceptions of gender and value. In terms of the sort of disciplinary comparisons discussed in Chapter 2, economists have in a sense "masculinized" the profession past the point of seeking to emulate actual practice in the physical and biological sciences. Standard practices in those fields seem to be still too applied and routine for economists' sensibilities. Economists have left the standards of the physical and biological sciences behind, in order to value in economic practice only those aspects derived from the yet more disengaged disciplines of "pure" mathematics and statistics.

The consequences of low status

This derogation of applied empirical analysis allows narrow formal rational choice theory to run the show. Chapter 6 demonstrated how rational choice theory has been allowed to direct empirical work about household equivalence scales in directions unhelpful for addressing the underlying policy issue.

As another example of interest to feminist policy concerns, consider Solomon Polachek's (1993) notion of how to deal with demand-side labor market discrimination. In this work he describes his own considerable efforts in gathering empirical information to explain why women's human capital choices result in lower wages. While he relies on empirical work to explain the supply side of the labor market, he apparently believes that theory without empirical work is sufficient for prescribing remedies for the demand side of the labor market. Explicit anti-discrimination policies, he implies, are unnecessary. Since Beckerian theory "shows" that discrimination can only exist in noncompetitive markets, Polachek's advises that "promoting economic competition is the greatest weapon in preventing discrimination" (1993: 14). Presumably, the work of the Equal Employment Opportunity Commission can be better accomplished just by letting the Federal Trade Commission do its job. Such examples of empirically unsupported but precise theories being allowed to trump strong but less precise empirical evidence are legion.

The consequences of overemphasis on rigor

Even when empirical work is taken seriously, the emphasis on formal testing, as contrasted to less formal information gathering, can hamper empirical progress.

Consider the standard approach to "testing for" the presence of labor market discrimination using wage data. This usually takes the form of regressing wages on a vector of job and human capital characteristics and a dummy variable representing sex. While such regressions can certainly be informative about the structure of wages, no sophisticated researcher will ever be convinced one way or another about discrimination on the basis of "tests" from such work, unless they already want to be. If the dummy variable representing sex has a negative and statistically significant coefficient, believers in impartial markets will argue that this is due to the omission of important variables measuring unobserved characteristics of men and women (e.g., ambition, energy level, etc.). If the researcher finds some way of measuring and including such a factor, the critic can always think up another one. If the dummy variable representing sex, on the other hand, fails to have a negative and significant coefficient, the researcher who believes there is discrimination in this market can always criticize the quality of the data or suggest that other omitted (or included) variables have created this result. But this is just the sort of point that Summers (1991) made about empirical macroeconomics: good empirical economics does not progress by way of formal tests of specific hypothesis. What we have in this disagreement is not a problem resolvable by classical hypothesis tests, but a case of those who hold the *a priori* belief that rational choice models of well-functioning labor markets represent real world phenomena, vs. those who are willing to accept the evidence of direct observation of actual attitudes and behavior. Evidence of discrimination is available by the boatload for many labor markets. Bergmann (1986) cites abundant evidence taken from court cases and laboratory studies (e.g., about differential evaluation of work by sex). Interview surveys, oral history studies, focus group studies, and historical reviews of personnel policies can be other sources of information. Studies of labor markets that are not hog-tied by adherence to a narrow definition of acceptable data and misled by the illusion of definitive "proof" will make (careful) use of such sources. This is not to say that further investigation of wage equations is futile; the investigation of the effects of sex on wages in disaggregate areas is still a worthwhile task whose results cannot always be predicted in advance, and such studies serve to refine and narrow the areas of disagreement. It is only to say that quality empirical work in general requires broader standards of evidence and has a less narrow view of knowledge formation.

Another example of the theoretical cart being allowed to pull the empirical horse, of interest to feminist policy concerns, is the work by Daniela Del Boca and Christopher Flinn (1992) on the way in which divorced mothers spend child support payments. These researchers found, using U.S. Consumer Expenditure Survey data, that the propensity of custodial mothers to spend on child-specific goods (such as children's clothing) was higher out of child support income than out of own income. This stylized fact could be important in thinking about the effectiveness of support on maintaining child welfare. Most noneconomists would, I assume, interpret this result as reflecting a greater perceived legitimacy of children's claims on this money *vis à vis* their mothers – not so, apparently, Del Boca and Flinn. While they acknowledge that feelings of "moral or legal obligation" could explain such patterns, they dismiss this hypothesis since such "preference shifts are *not useful from the point of view of testing*" (1992: 11; emphasis added). While their result may be useful in ways other than what they intended, they see themselves not as looking for patterns in household spending – which would be a pragmatic, informal endeavor – but as testing an hypothesis derived from a formal micro-model – in this case, that parents continue to be involved in a (Nash) bargaining game after marital dissolution.

The lowest of the low

Hierarchies also exist between fields of economic study, which then carry over to empirical applications as well. One consequence of the public/private dualism that puts higher value on industry and government than on families is that investigation into household consumption patterns is held in rather low regard. While the term "microeconomics" is in general taken to apply to producers and consumers alike, in fact the term "applied microeconomics" is often taken to refer only to the producer side, and serves as a synonym for industrial organization. Specialized journals within the profession exist for the study of households on their labor-supply side, but studies on the consumption side have to be considered of general enough importance to be appropriate for the more general journals, or be fitted awkwardly into labor economics journals, or be published outside of the profession in journals devoted to marketing research or consumer advocacy.

CONCLUSION

In macroeconomics, and in any field of economics that pretends to have something to say about the economic world we live in, economic practice would be much improved by a decreased emphasis on the technique of "musing" (Bergmann 1987) and an increased emphasis on "hobnobbing with one's data" (Strober 1987). Such prescriptions echo the much older advice from Richard T. Ely about "getting down into this life and studying it carefully" (Ely 1938: 156; also see Chapter 4). Barbara Bergmann (1987), who sees the appropriate methods for economics as being more like those of anthropology than mathematics, predicts that when "we leave off musing and regression running on secondhand data, I predict we will be amazed at the doctrines which fall" (1987: 194). Such empirical work is not a-theoretical, but rather, as Summers (1991: 140) put it, starts "from a theoretic viewpoint not a straitjacket."

Part III

SPECIFIC DEFENSES

9

TO ECONOMISTS: WHY
FEMINIST?

IS THIS JUST ANOTHER HETERODOX CRITIQUE?

This book is not, of course, the first to suggest that economics should be flexible, attentive to context, humanistic and rich, as well as hard, logical, scientific and precise; or that the notion of Economic Man is seriously deficient as a model of actual human behavior in relation to nature and society; or that economics should concern itself more with concrete issues of provisioning related to the actual social and natural environment and less with abstract analysis of hypothetical choice. While the core of economics has remained firmly planted in the seventeenth century, the rest of the world has moved on. Periodic criticisms have been lobbed at economics, and at masculine-identified aspects of scientific thought in general, by both insiders and outsiders who, quite clearly, see the deficiencies of current practice.

Many of these criticisms concerning the narrowness of the field have been raised, for example, in presidential addresses to the American Economic Association by Richard T. Ely (1936), Kenneth Boulding (1969), Wassily Leontief (1971), John Kenneth Galbraith (1973), and Robert Gordon (1976) and in recent high-profile speeches by distinguished economists Alan Blinder (1988) and Henry J. Aaron (1994). Previous chapters have drawn explicitly on related critiques by economists such as Donald McCloskey, Lawrence Summers and Thomas Mayer. I have also regarded with interest (though not always with total agreement) the work of, for example, Robert Frank (1988) on rationality and emotion; of Herman Daly and John B. Cobb (1989) on "persons-in-community;" of Philip Mirowski (1988) on the implications of Cartesian thought; of Vernon Dixon (1970, 1977) on an "Afro-centered" view of economics; and of Jack Amariglio (1988) on postmodernism and economics. Marxists, Institutionalists, Austrians, Post-Keynesians, and "socio-" economists have kept up an unrelenting criticism of neoclassical assumptions. Yet mainstream economics seems to have stayed its course quite well in spite of the onslaught. What does feminist theory have to add that is new? Is there any reason to believe that the feminist critique could be effective in bringing about improvement?

WHY GENDER IS IMPORTANT

As a devil's advocate position, suppose we argue for the moment that gender, or more specifically, the protection of a particular "masculine" conception of economics, is not an important factor in these internal debates within the discipline. Suppose that these are all real debates, but I am making a mountain out of a molehill by drawing out masculine/ feminine associations. The major counter-argument to this comes directly from the sociology of knowledge: does not this argument also suggest that the exclusion of women from economics is of negligible importance? If sexism, on the social and intellectual levels, is simply incidental and suitable as the subject of drawing- (or seminar-) room jokes, then the debate about the definition of economics can presumably be carried on without any discussion of gender, and even entirely by men. If on the other hand sexism (manifested, among other ways, in the exclusion of women from the community of scholars who define economics) is a pervasive social fact, is it not likely that it has had some influence on the construction of the intellectual foundations of the discipline? Note that my argument does not rest, as does Donald McCloskey's (1988), on the claim that women think differently, and so would "bring" something different to economics. Most female economists I know do research that is indistinguishable from that of their male colleagues. Rather I claim that it is systematic sexism – the systematic devaluation of women as part of a systematic devaluation of "the feminine" on many levels – that is the most important link between women and the disparaged ways of knowing. The historic exclusion of women, combined with evidence of the one-sided recent development of economics is, I believe, at least suggestive of the idea that the protection of the "masculinity" of economics has played a role in the construction of the discipline.

To put it bluntly, I argue that much of the staying-power of the neoclassical hegemony is subtly tied to the sting of the insult, "sissy." No one wants to be thought "soft" in one's work, since (perhaps subconsciously) by implication this is to be thought "feminine." One might also wonder if generational effects are behind the evolution of ever-rising standards of technical expertise. An informal survey of presidential addresses and the like by distinguished senior economists suggests that many such critics of overemphasis on sophisticated technique were in their younger days among those leading the charge to greater formalization and mathematization. Perhaps the sociology of the profession includes a need of the intellectual "sons" to prove their masculinity by one-upmanship over their intellectual "fathers." None of the gender associations need to go on at a conscious level, of course. In fact, once such biases are established, institutional inertia may be sufficient to keep the discipline moving down the masculine-biased path, even if the majority of practitioners were no longer to associate masculinity with value in other areas of their lives.

Feminist scholarship suggests that fundamental concepts of Western thought – especially hierarchical dualisms of reason over nature, and separation over connection – are fundamentally tied into a gender ideology that also ranks men over women. While neoclassical economics displays allegiance to this ideology in an extreme form, suggested alternatives to neoclassical economics may also, by not examining deeply enough the sources of their categories of thought, display some of the same biases. The analysis set out in Chapter 2 suggests that undeserved emphasis has been placed, in economics, on the left-hand column of Table 2.1 (e.g., on markets vs. families, and self-interest vs. other-interest, etc.). The solution I have proposed is to use our cognitive capabilities to think beyond the either–or, center–margin structure presented in such dualistic contrasts. The solution is to rethink the entire diagram; to examine what is valuable about each concept, and what harm comes of emphasizing either side to the exclusion of the other. Most other adaptations or critiques of mainstream practice, I will argue, recognize only parts of the problem and/or suggest less satisfactory solutions.

SOME TAKE FROM THE RIGHT-HAND-SIDE ONLY SELECTIVELY

Some innovations in economics have challenged some, but not all, of the dualisms that define the discipline. An affirmative action approach that simply encourages more women to enter economics, without expecting any change in the discipline, for example, makes only an isolated (though important) stab at changing the discipline's culture of sexism. The "New Home Economists," of whom Gary Becker is the leader, have brought family issues into economics, while leaving the methods and key assumptions largely unchanged. Such an innovation is something of a mixed bag for feminists: while it makes issues historically of special concern to women legitimate at least at the margins of economics, the literature has in fact largely formalized and reinforced outdated assumptions about male and female roles.

Modifications of strict "economic man" assumptions, such as the addition of "altruism" through the construct of altruistic preferences or interdependent utility, or such as limitations put on rationality, can be grafted on to the basic model without threatening its core. The temporary nature of such grafts, however, is evident in the following quote:

> A perplexing phenomenon of modern society is the significant role of cooperation . . . Understanding how it comes about and can be sustained are major research questions to social scientists. The challenge to economists has been to explain cooperative behavior as being consistent with individual rationality.
>
> (Harrington, 1989)

Note that cooperative behavior is seen as a puzzle, while individuality and competition is the unquestioned base. The next model, unless cooperation is exactly the question at issue, will no doubt revert to the core model.

Other critiques, such as Donald McCloskey's (1985) work on rhetoric and Arjo Klamer's (1989) work on interpretive economics, look to both columns as guidelines for method, but say less about the domain of economics or about key assumptions. Others challenge the key assumptions of economic theory, such as the autonomy of agents vs. their social nature (e.g. Thurow 1988; Solow 1990), but neglect to apply these to women or families. Thurow, for example, applies notions of social nature only to the market side: "we are social producers," he recognizes, but "we are individual consumers in nuclear families" (1988).

Other major schools of economics, such as Marxism, Institutionalism, Post-Keynesianism, etc. also reject the neoclassical dualisms in specific ways. While feminists can learn from them, they and all schools are also possible subjects of cross-critique (see, e.g., Folbre 1993b; Jennings 1993).

AN EXAMPLE: "HUMANISTIC" ECONOMICS

As an example of cross-critique, consider the "humanistic" or "socio-" economics proposed by Mark A. Lutz and Kenneth Lux (1988). Their major criticism of neoclassical economics – that its focus on rational, autonomous and (especially) self-interested agents leaves it inadequate – has many parallels with the feminist critique. As in the feminist view, Lutz and Lux see humans as reasonable, instead of capable of only strictly logical rationality; as embedded in communities, instead of as always dealing with others at arms' length; as capable of action that reflects connection to others, instead of action that reflects only self-interest. A feminist reading such work, however, may be struck by instances in which the "humanistic" world view has much in common with that of mainstream economics. Lutz and Lux question some but not all of the dualisms concerning the nature of the agent, and leave the subject matter firmly on the "public" side.

Lutz and Lux's interpretation of "humanistic" economics builds on the work of Abraham Maslow in psychology. Their alternative to neoclassical "economic man" is a view of humans as incorporating a "higher self" and a "lower self." The higher self is characterized by reasonableness, principled behavior, altruism, objectivity, and transpersonal goals, while the lower self is characterized by economic rationality, instrumental behavior, selfishness, subjectivity, and purely personal goals (1988: 17). The lower self includes interests related to our "animal" existence, ruled by "passions or desires," in the "kingdom of nature," while the higher self transcends these to enter into the "kingdom of reason" (ibid.: 106–7). The basic duality of the human being is, according to Maslow, "the predicament, of being simultaneously merely creaturely and godlike, strong and weak, limited and unlimited, merely animal and animal-transcending . . . yearning for perfection and yet afraid of it, being a worm and also a hero" (Maslow, in Lutz and Lux 1988: 16).

Feminists have had good reason, however, to be suspicious of these hierarchical dualisms. Women have historically been associated with the deprecated "nature" or "animal" side of the mind/nature dualism and the deprecated "emotion" side of reason/emotion dualism. Women, nature, and emotion have all come out the worse for it. Rather than treating these hierarchical dualisms as somehow reflecting something intrinsic to reality, feminist scholars have questioned them (Chapters 1, 2 and 3). An acceptance of the reason/nature hierarchy also puts Lutz and Lux's definition of economics on an unsteady base. They argue against defining economics by the rational choice model instead of by its "subject matter" (1988: 179). But really, aren't subjects such as production and consumption – much less poverty – really rather grubby, since they have to do with our "lower" animal existence and instrumental activities? Isn't dealing with choice a much cleaner and more important activity, since reason is part of the "higher" self? So would go the reasoning from the hierarchical dualism.

Another aspect of their hierarchical dualism that feminists have called into question is whether altruism is always good. Lutz and Lux define altruism, in agreement with Auguste Comte, as "the discipline and eradication of self-centered desire, and a life devoted to the good of others." (1988: 109). The overcoming of self-interest in order to act also for the interests of others has been for centuries a major theme of both religious and ethical discussions. But is it free of gender bias? While most theologians and ethicists have seen the primary manifestation of "sin" for traditional males as overblown selfishness, some have argued that the primary manifestation of "sin" for traditional females is overblown self-abnegation (see discussion in C. Keller 1986, especially p. 12; Gilligan 1982: chapter 5; Hampton 1993). Males tend to fail by becoming individuated selves too separate from others; females are more likely to fail by not developing individual selfhood at all. Does not the definition of altruism given above describe for some the ideal traditional wife and mother, who has no identity of her own apart from her husband and children? Yet such a person has usually not been seen as particularly virtuous, either because (as for women) such devotion is thought to be "only natural," or because it is recognized that a lack of individual identity also means, in an ethical or spiritual sense, a corresponding erasure of individual responsibility. Lutz and Lux's hierarchy of self-development, from self-interest to other-interest, represents largely the traditionally masculine path of ethical development. If the ideal person has both an individual identity and a sense of solidarity with others, feminist research reminds us that guard must also be kept against a too thorough "eradication" of the self.

These points can be seen in terms of the diagram introduced in Chapter 1. The argument for increased unselfishness is based on a hierarchy:

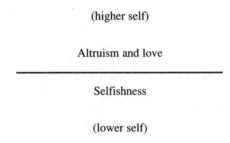

(higher self)

Altruism and love

Selfishness

(lower self)

A diagram on the relationship of self- and other-interest that is informed by feminist theory is:

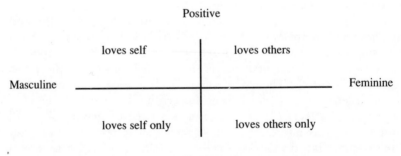

Positive

loves self | loves others

Masculine | Feminine

loves self only | loves others only

Negative

Instead of a hierarchy of other-interest over self-interest, this diagram suggests the virtues of a balance.

What would the "humanistic economics" analysis lose, if it dropped the notion that some needs and attitudes, like the needs for self-actualization and transpersonal connection and the attitude of other-interest, are "higher," while others, like material needs and an attitude of self-interest, are "lower"? I do not think anything would be lost, and much clarity would be gained. As I suggested in Chapter 5, it may sometimes be helpful to think of human welfare as having three dimensions: agency, dealing with the locus of control over one's life; affiliation, dealing with our need for attachment to other people; and living standards, dealing with bodily requirements and satisfactions. No one aspect takes precedence over the other, nor can any one be reduced to the other. Rather than imposing a higher/lower dualism among these different aspects of human life, we can think about what is higher and lower within each dimension. The left-hand side of the above diagram, for example, suggests the higher (assertive, paying attention to own interests) and lower (selfish) levels of agency; the right-hand side gives the higher (concerned about others) and lower (dissolving into others) levels of affiliation. We could do the same for living standards: fulfillment of what we need is on the higher level, while seeking fulfillment through excessive material accumulation fits on the lower level.[1] In every case, the lower level entries are related to the higher level qualities, as their perverted form when they are taken to extremes. The "humanistic economics" approach could be improved by some distancing from Maslow's simple dualisms.

A masculine perspective is also demonstrated in the work of Lutz and Lux in a concentration on market activities and masculine notions of identity, to the neglect of home activities and consideration of traditional feminine ways of forming identity. Economic production in the home is, as in neoclassical economics, largely neglected. Since the role of childhood and family is ignored, Lutz and Lux's "dual-self" is no less a Hobbesian "mushroom man" than the neoclassical agent, though he may be a different variety of mushroom.

While the "humanistic" and feminist approaches start with the same criticisms of the neoclassical model, feminist scholarship suggests that the "humanistic" approach of Lutz and Lux still retains too much in common with the mainstream ideology.

---

[1] I do not include the issue of gender connotations in the present exposition of the material dimension of welfare. While I believe that an investigation of such connotations can often be very illuminating, this does not mean that gender has to be dragged into each and every discussion.

SOME CRITIQUES REVERSE OR OVERTHROW THE COLUMNS OF TABLE 2.1

If economics were to take its cues from other disciplines, it might also consider the notions of "gynocentric" (woman-centered) science or feminist "Postmodernist" approaches that have been discussed there. The so-called woman-centered approach rejects all of what it perceives as male-centered science, including norms of objectivity and analytical inquiry, in favor of completely distinct assumptions and methods. It retains the sort of dualisms outlined in Table 2.1 (page 22), only switching the headings so that the "feminine" side becomes the core. This serves to reinforce, rather than break down, sex stereotypes.

The Postmodernist approach uses techniques of literary criticism to "deconstruct" traditional understandings. Ulla Grapard (1992), Lee Levin (1993), Gillian Hewitson (1993) and Rhonda Williams (1993) are among feminist economists who have explored a Postmodernist approach. Jack Amariglio (1988) and Jane Rossetti (1993) have written (with greater or lesser enthusiasm) about the contributions Postmodernism could make to economics. Deconstructionists in the tradition of Jacques Derrida and Michael Foucault seek to dismantle all claims to objectivity and universal, timeless knowledge. Each side of a dualism such as those in Table 2.1, according to deconstructionists, maintains its meaning only in relation to the opposite concept. The concepts themselves have no essential meaning. In deconstructionist thought, language does not convey meaning but rather creates it through such binary oppositions. As there is no meaning outside of language, there are no objects or ideas that are fundamental, eternal or universally true. Language reflects the time, place, and worldview of the community. To "deconstruct" a text is to show how a particular discourse poses as universal and objective – to show how the subordinate sides of the dualisms are implicit in the argument and how dominance is created. Once a text that has been purported to expound on subjects universal and objective has been exposed in all its particularity and subjectivity, however, the contribution of deconstruction ends. Deconstruction does not offer a new way of evaluating the adequacy of knowledge claims: it offers only "endless deferral or play" (Poovey 1988).

One can accept much of the Postmodern critique, however, without accepting the full, radically subjectivist Postmodern prescription. Much of the analysis of this book has been postmodernist – small "p", lowbrow, meaning "after modernism" – in spirit, deconstructing the binary dualisms in Table 2.1 even though it eschews the vocabulary of the highbrow literary criticism. Yes, modernist social science has made false claims to universality. Yes, what we claim to know about the world is mediated by language, culture, and society. Yes, binary dualisms like masculine/feminine are cognitive patterns that need deconstructing. But, no, this does not imply that the world is actually "constituted by" language, or that one knowledge claim is as good as any another, or that the category "woman" is illegitimate and meaningless. Instead of flipping from radical objectivism to radical subjectivism, the analysis presented in this book (especially Chapter 3) suggests that the objective/subjective dualism itself be rethought; instead of setting gendered bodies aside in a focus on free play in language, this analysis suggests that gendered embodiment be taken very seriously.

CONCLUSION

A major cause of the systematic biases that have grown up in economics may be a historical fear of the feminine, carried forward into current practice by continuing cultural sexism as well as by institutional inertia. Failure to recognize this point, and consistently work out its implications, may also help to explain why the various attempts at modification or replacement of the neoclassical paradigm have been so far largely unsuccessful. The search for a better economics may be intimately tied with the feminist effort to rid society at large of its deep-rooted sexism.

This is not to say that feminist theory offers a perfect, "ideology-free" standpoint from which all other approaches must be judged. At the very least, class and race differences also need to be addressed. To reiterate, a feminist approach does not rely on a premise that "women think differently." But a feminist approach does start to widen the discourse, in a way that enhances objectivity. And a feminist approach does open to practitioners of economic science, whether male or female, a new way of looking at our categories of thought and the value we place on different models and methods.

10

TO FEMINISTS: HOW FEMINIST?

RELATION TO OTHER FEMINIST PROJECTS

Chapter 1 offered a pictorial representation of how a feminist re-visioning of the relationships between constructions of "masculine" and "feminine" might function. I have found this picture, or simple model, to be helpful in organizing the ideas of hierarchies, polarities, dualisms, "differences," and "complementarities" I have encountered in my reading of the works of other feminist scholars and in evaluating various projects that have been proposed as goals for feminist scholarship. The usefulness of a simple model is not that it incorporates all aspects of reality, but that in highlighting selected aspects of the subject of concern it may help us to organize our thinking. Yet this construction has met with opposition from various feminist scholars. In this chapter I seek to meet those objections.

The problem of "difference" has received much attention from feminists. We observe that men and women in our culture often act differently and have different experiences. Should feminists deny or downplay current differences between men and women, suggesting that they are entirely cultural artifacts that should be overcome? Or should feminists acknowledge and even celebrate differences between men and women, whether assumed to be based in biology or in experience? Feminist analysis often tends to swing back and forth between the extremes of trying to erase difference – what Evelyn Fox Keller (1986a) refers to as "counting to one" – and emphasizing difference, although perhaps in a "feminist" fashion, as in revaluing "women's experience" – what Keller refers to as "counting to two." This conflict between erasure of and emphasis of difference has also been discussed as the conflict between "minimalist" and "maximalist" feminism by Catherine R. Stimpson (cited in Bernard 1987); between "beta bias" and "alpha bias" by Rachel T. Hare-Mustin and Jeanne Marecek (1988); between "individualist" and "relational" feminism by Karen Offen (1988); and between "sex neutrality" and "sex polarity" by Jean Bethke Elshtain (1987). The emphasis on difference has also sometimes been been called "cultural feminism" (see citations in Alcoff 1988). Hester Eisenstein and Alice Jardine (1985), Mary Crawford (1989), Helen Weinreich-Haste (1986), Genevieve Lloyd (1984: especially 103–10), and Susan Bordo (1990) present other examples of discussions among feminists about the problem of "difference."

Keller suggests that we need "a different kind of language, reflecting a higher dimensionality in our landscape – neither homogeneous nor divided, spacious enough to enable multiplicity to survive without degenerating into opposition" (Keller 1987: 48). This is what I tried to do in Chapter 1 – in the most literal sense of "higher dimensionality." The gender–value compass turns the bipolar difference relationship masculine–good/feminine–bad into a four-pole, four-cell picture of masculine/feminine and good/bad. One difference can be seen as not requiring that one pole be "higher" than the other, gender difference becomes less scary, and the need to see it erased dissipates. Once it is recognized that the connection between gender difference and biological sex difference is often only by very tenuous metaphor, on the other hand, we are less likely to overemphasize sexual difference.

COMPARED TO GENDER NEUTRALITY

Does this approach reify gender distinctions? Perhaps instead of dealing with gender categories we would be better off training ourselves into working without them. My vision of the feminist project differs sharply from that of feminist intellectuals who would like to remove the categories of gender from our thinking – that is, get rid of sexism by getting rid of difference. The danger of using gender categories, from this point of view, is the very real tendency of categories of femininity and masculinity to become reified, that is, to come to represent a presumed essence of femaleness or maleness instead of a culturally and historically variable technique of cognitive patterning. Sandra Bem, for example, has argued that "human behaviors and personality attributes should cease to have gender, and society should stop projecting gender into situations irrelevant to genitalia" (Bem 1981: 363).

While recognizing the dangers of reification, I suspect that creation of such a "gender aschematic" society is an impossibility in a society that is recognizably human. I agree with Catherine Keller that "we never grow beyond or above but always with or through our gender identities" (1986: 4). If gender is so deeply embedded in our minds that it can even serve to organize our thinking about cats and dogs and odd and even numbers (Chapter 1), I see little hope for rooting it out. I see more hope in trying to break the associations between gender difference and hierarchical opposition and between gender difference and unexamined assumptions of biological determinism. I would locate the positive aspect of the idea of "de-gendering" not at the level of eliminating gender categories as a cognitive patterning device, but, first, as the assertion that gender categories are irrelevant in making judgments about whether something is good or bad, full or lacking, healthy or perverse, and, second, as the recognition that the gender categories of feminine and masculine are only linked to biological categories of female and male through a complex web of increasingly tenuous metaphorical association.

Since this point has been misunderstood in the past (Elliot 1994) it is worthwhile highlighting the way in which I understand gender. My assertion that it would be foolish to try to eliminate gender is based on my understanding of gender as a cognitive organizer, very much in a linguistic sense. Gender distinctions are cognitive organizers built on an experience of the biological distinction between male and female. The recognition of gender as a cognitive organizer in no way compromises my opposition to an oppressive sex-gender system, in which individuals of each sex are forced into culturally defined gender roles. Proponents of gender neutrality believe that elimination of gender – that is, elimination of all meaning (other than perhaps narrowly reproductive) of terms men/women, masculine/feminine – is a prerequisite for a non-sexist society. I disagree. I would like instead to make a clear distinction between the projects of gender neutrality and anti-sexism. There are several ways in which I believe a campaign for gender neutrality actually undermines the more important project.

It is already well established in the literature on sexism and language that gender neutrality can actually serve sexist, instead of non-sexist, purposes (Frank and Treichler 1989: 17–18). For example, relabeling wife battering as gender-neutral "spousal abuse" hides the predominant source of the violence. Referring to a class of people as "non-pregnant persons" has allowed for interpretations of disability law in ways detrimental to women (Okin 1989: 11). While I doubt that many feminists believe that gender neutrality is by itself sufficient (as opposed to necessary) for non-sexism, many people who have no interest in examining the depths of sexism are more than eager to make this confusion. "The tax code is written in gender-inclusive language," some economists have claimed, "so therefore charges that it is sexist must be unfounded." Gender neutrality may also be rejected by many as a goal. For some reason, the argument that the Equal Rights Amendment would make men and women use the same restrooms hit a nerve among portions of the public during ERA debates, sidetracking what should have been a debate about sexism and turning it into a reaction against gender neutrality. *Disassociating* non-sexism and gender neutrality is often a necessary first step in starting a meaningful conversation.

One might also wonder if pervasive gender-based grammar is corre-lated, cross-culturally, with especially pervasive distinctions between the sexes on a social level. Do cultures which have gender-neutral languages also have less sexist social structures? According to linguists, this does not seem to be the case (Corbett 1991). For example, while many Asian languages are completely lacking in grammatical gender, one can hardly argue that the cultures are lacking social gender distinctions and sexism.

The feasibility of gender neutrality also seems to me to be widely in doubt. All feminists agree that people should be freed of sexist stereo-types and behavioral and occupational expectations – the "policing" aspect of the sex-gender system. Yet many people – feminists and potential feminists among them – find the notion that all systematic differences between girls and boys, and men and women, are the result of gender-biased cultural pressures to be a bit on the untenable side. I believe that what we need here is a slightly more sophisticated conception of gender association.

Consider gender association as taking place at three different levels. The first, what we might call "direct," refers to masculine/feminine distinctions in chromosomes or genitalia. I see no reason to seek to overcome such categorization. The second level, or "correlative," refers to characteristics that are statistically associated with sex difference, such as secondary anatomical and (limited) behavioral regularities. Here I think the non-sexist approach should be to become more sophisticated about how we use these associations. If 60 percent of women have trait Z (e.g. wide hips) but 80 percent of men do not have it, Z may be labeled a "feminine" characteristic. But this still means that 40 percent of women are "not feminine" and 20 percent of men are "feminine." The labeling only becomes dangerous when it is confused with value (i.e., feminine is inferior) or with necessary traits of individuals (e.g., "real men" do not have feminine traits). A third level is "metaphorical" gender association, where gender is associated with classes of ob-jects and abstract principles on the basis of increasingly tenuous ties to sex difference. Such associations have been the major topic of this book.

I do not mean to imply that training ourselves and the rest of society to disassociate correlative gender and metaphorical gender from value on the one hand, and from expectations for individuals on the other, is likely to be easy; only that feminist efforts are better applied to this project than to one of eliminating gender as a means of cognitive structuring. If gender becomes a cognitive organizer because of the way that language and the mind develop, starting in early childhood, then gender neutrality requires the active suppression of sexual difference as a salient aspect of human experience, especially the experience of children. The absolutely strict focus on "genitalia – and only genitalia" in

143

discussions of gender with children suggested by Bem (1983: 613) for example, must mean that in addition to teaching children to ignore cultural correlates such as clothing or hair style, one must also teach them to ignore what their own vision tells them are anatomical correlates: regularities in the distribution of voice pitch, facial hair, height, hip width, presence of breasts, shoulder width, fineness of features, muscle definition, propensity to baldness, etc. Perhaps some people yearn for Marge Piercy's (1976) fictional gender-free utopia, in which both primary and secondary sexual characteristics have been cleansed of any differentiating significance. In Piercy's novel, reproduction is through artificial wombs, hormone therapy allows men to breast feed, and the key character has a body shape that leads to gender confusion. Society could perhaps develop the technology for such a transition, but in a sexist society would we want to encourage that research? For every dream of such reproductive technology leading to a feminist utopia, there is a corresponding nightmare of it leading to a society in which women are finally dispensable, and so dispensed with.

While complete gender neutrality has a certain appeal as being perhaps the most surgically clean way of eliminating sexism, and may appeal to some for its "radical" pose, I think a far more radical approach is to think about new notions of justice and equality that can be applied in the face of systematic human diversity. Sexual dimorphism leads to gender being used as a cognitive organizer. Our use of gender categories often reflects our sexism, but this use of gender categories should not be mistaken as the cause of sexism. The cause of sexism is not sexual dimorphism, just as the cause of racism does not lie in differences in physiognomy or bloodline. Both forms of oppression come from the drive of one group to dominate another. A world without sex or race distinctions could not be sexist or racist, it is true, but it could be just as structured by oppression by using other categorizations as the dividing factors. A world with acknowledged variety in sex and race need not be oppressive, if the distinctions are not used as a basis for domination.

COMPARED TO GYNOCENTRISM

Does my approach give too much advantage to masculine concerns? Perhaps we should forget about the left side of the gender–value compass and try instead for a "gynocentric" society based on "women's values." From this perspective, the danger of my gender–value compass, which is more "human-centered" or inclusive, is that without adequate reconstruction of what it means to be "feminine" old sexist assumptions about passivity and submission might continue to define the feminine side of the picture. (Some critics from this camp might add that the whole idea of diagraming gender is "too analytical" – i.e., too masculine.) The dangers I see in the gynocentric approach are a possible lack of distinction between feminine–positive and feminine–negative attributes, a disabling repression of masculine–positive attributes, and a reification of the "women are feminine; men are masculine" dichotomy. What I see as a positive aspect of the gynocentric view is its serious attempt to find, name, and revalue the feminine–positive attributes about which, at this point, we can barely speak.

My gender–value compass has actually been confused with gynocentrism by some critics (Elliot 1994), based on a reading that emphasizes only my addition of the F + term. Such a reading of my approach as a simple "revaluing of the feminine" is severely distorting, however, as it leaves out the F − (dangers of extreme femininity) and M + (benefits of balanced masculinity) terms.

My work may be compared to that of another scholar whose work has often been interpreted as "revaluing the feminine." Carol Gilligan (1987b) also sets out contrasts of separation- and connection-related terms, and suggests a graphical metaphor to capture their relation. Gilligan notes (1987b: 90) that "independence" and "isolation" are both "opposites of the word 'dependence'" and suggests that "since dependence connotes the experience of connection, its axes extend along the two coordinates of relationships – leading in one direction to independence and in the other to isolation." In such an analysis she captures three of the four cells in my related gender–value compass. What is missing from her metaphor, however, is the feminine–negative term, i.e., the equivalent to "soluble" or "engulfed." Such a term ("selfless") finally appears on page 92 of Gilligan's work. Looking at her work using the gender–value compass suggests that an important term is missing from her earlier graphical metaphor (and from "gynocentric" work in general), and shows how all of the concepts Gilligan (eventually) presents might be assumed into a single metaphor.[1]

COMPARED TO FEMINIST POSTMODERNISM

Another way of getting out of the minimalist/maximalist dilemma has been suggested by feminists such as Joan W. Scott (1988), Mary Poovey (1988), Linda Alcoff (1988), and Linda J. Nicholson (1990) who use the approach of deconstruction, associated with the work of Jacques Derrida and Michael Foucault. I believe the goals of the two projects are the same: if I understand the deconstructionist vocabulary correctly, Mary Poovey's project of finding a way to "dismantle binary logic and

[1] For a wide-ranging discussion of the problem of feminine-identified "selflessness" for moral theory, see Jean Hampton (1993).

deconstruct identity" is what I would express in my own chosen vocabulary as finding a way to explode simple dualisms and move beyond unidimensionality. The philosophical bases are, however, quite different. By drawing on Lakoff and Johnson's idea of cognition as based in metaphors, one avoids having to adapt to the baggage of radical relativism that some feminists have argued comes along with certain strains of deconstructionist philosophy.[2] The identification of the basis of metaphor as experience, and especially physical experience, also puts human physical bodies explicitly at the heart of the analysis (Johnson 1987). The extent to which "the body" figures into deconstructionist thought is in dispute.[3] The most significant distinction between my approach and the deconstructionist one, however, comes in the pragmatic question of what one is supposed to use as a substitute for binary opposition. The deconstructionist answer is "endless deferral or play" (Poovey 1988: 52) or the "constant vigilant suspicion of all determinate readings of culture and a partner aesthetic of ceaseless textual play" (Bordo 1990: 142). In contrast, my answer is more simply, and provisionally, "use a more complex metaphor."

My approach is thus both more pessimistic, and more optimistic, about human cognitive abilities. The deconstructionist literature seems to assume that all its readers have the time and inclination to become versed in its vocabulary and rules through extensive scholarly study of contemporary literary criticism; either that, or it assumes that theorizing best be left to the literary élite. I doubt the practicality of the first option and deplore the parochialism of the second. On the other hand, while deconstructionist thought recognizes that undimensional binary oppositions are basic conceptual building blocks, it does not recognize that we all learn, easily and at a young age, to handle more than one dimension at a time. In any movement through space, we have to deal simultaneously with up/down, left/right, and forward/back: even though we might in some contexts draw on metaphorically constructed links between up-right-forward(-good) and down-left-back(-bad), we certainly do not choose to make use of these particular metaphors all the time; if we did we would never be able to order our movements. Moving spatially, we can deal with the fact that "up" and "left" are related but that the relation is not oppositional. I believe we can train ourselves to perceive the same sort of more complex relation between "good" and "female."

---

[2] See the essays by Seyla Benhabib, Susan Bordo, and Nancy Hartsock in Nicholson (1990).
[3] See the essays by Jane Flax (especially p. 48) and Susan Bordo (especially pp. 142–5) in Nicholson (1990).

RELATION TO OTHER FORMS OF DIFFERENCE

I came to writing this book by thinking about gender in the contemporary, white, intellectual, culture in which I am located. The gender–value compass was created as a tool for understanding gender and value in this context. Now created, can this tool be used for other purposes? As I have already mentioned, the content of the gender–value compass will change as gender is analyzed in different contexts. For example, the metaphorical association of femininity with "soft" (which I used earlier) applies much more to white women of the middle or upper classes than to women of color or to women who do manual labor. In a different context, the content would be different. I hesitate to assert just what the content would be in other contexts or to extend the framework to analysis of race or class or other forms of difference myself, because I suspect the process of putting content to the diagram is both as important as the final content itself and strongly tied to experience. The purpose of the diagram is to increase clarity of thinking and thus empower people at the bottom of the old hierarchies – to create a cognitive space for finding value in the previously devalued and for creating new definitions of identity and knowledge.[4]

As a tool for thinking, the diagram may be useful wherever an existing hierarchy seems to leave one with only the choices of assimilation (the "counting to one" mentioned in the introduction) or of separatism (the "counting to two" of the introduction). While I have concentrated on the positive complementarities possible in looking at gender, consider the following by bell hooks, in which she talks about experience of race, region, and class:

> Faced with the choice of assimilating or returning to my roots, I would catch the first train home. There is another more difficult . . . choice, that is to decide to maintain values and traditions that emerge from a working-class Southern black folk experience while incorporating meaningful knowledge gained in other locations, even in those hierarchical spaces of privilege.
>
> (hooks 1990: 90)

What is good in each way of being? What should be kept from the one identity and what should be added from the other? On the other hand, what parts of each identity have been perverted by relations of

---

[4] This is not to excuse us from also examining our positions at the top of other hierarchies (as educated people who can afford to read books, at the least), but only to indicate the modest nature of the tool proposed. The "compass" is an instrument for thinking about the kind of social change we want; actually bringing about that change involves more hard work.

oppression? What should one discard from the one identity or be suspicious of in the other? Perhaps the notion of value as a separate dimension from race, class, ethnicity, or sexual preference, as well as from gender, can, along with the concepts of "complementarity," "lack," and "perversion," aid in clarifying these choices.

Seen in this more abstract context, my diagram is obviously de-centering in a postmodernist sense (using the word in its general, "after-modernism" meaning). "Essentialism" gives way to recognition of agency in the formation of identity, and all forms of privilege (including those enjoyed by feminists) may be called on the carpet and required to prove their worth or be unmasked. But, in contrast to a strain in the deconstructionist variant of postmodernism, the recognition of multiple and (somewhat) fluid identities does not necessarily imply that group identities are meaningless. To push my diagram one last step, consider one uneasy dualism that appears in some discussions of feminist theory: deconstructionist "difference" versus political solidarity. The positive aspects of deconstructionist writing are sometimes described as the investigation of new ways of "self-creation" and the critique of "uni-versalism" or "essentialism" that this recognition of individual agency implies (Rorty 1989; Fraser and Nicholson 1990; hooks 1990). On the other hand, feminists (and others) have raised the fear that the emphasis on difference may degenerate into a thoroughgoing individualism and political conservatism (Poovey 1988; Bordo 1990; Fraser and Nicholson 1990; Hartsock 1990). A very simple diagram may help to shed light on the relationships among universalism, solidarity, individualism, and rela-tivism by examining the different ways one might compare oneself to another human being:

Positive

distinct	similar

---

disjunctive	same

Negative

Starting at the bottom right, do we see others as the same, completely lacking in characteristics that would distinguish them from ourselves? This is false universalism and perhaps the failing of a too enthusiastic push for "sisterhood" in some episodes of feminism. Do we view others as disjunctive, that is, completely lacking in similarity? This overemphasis on differences leads to radical relativism and is a failing of a too-extreme form of postmodernist thought. But can we see others as similar? This is a basis for solidarity. And can we see others as distinct? This is a basis for respecting differences.

CONCLUSION

I offer my diagram of gender and value as a provisional tool. The structure offers one possible way to organize one's thoughts in the effort to "count past two." I do not present it as a finished product or as a structure that presumes to incorporate all possible aspects of gender and "difference." I see its main function as a sort of safety net that prevents one who is primed to thinking in binary oppositions from lapsing back into simple dualistic thinking. I hope that the gender–value compass is both simple enough to be readily understood and remembered and just rich enough to provide a small beginning toward a deeper understanding of gender. If it helps in a particular context, then use it; if it does not, then discard it. In terms of the content of the examples I have used to illustrate the diagrams, it would be a severe misinterpretation of my intent to take these as representing any unchangeable "essences" of femininity or masculinity. In fact, I would expect substantial disagreement over exactly what belongs in each quadrant when one looks at concepts from different historical, cultural, or personal perspectives. It is the underlying structure that is important. The structure allows simultaneous conceptualization of gender, value judgment, and difference without conflation of gender with hierarchy and antagonism.

EPILOGUE

Feminism does indeed have something to say about the objectivity of economics. By adopting a cultural value system that puts undue emphasis on masculine-associated traits and experiences, a concern for objectivity has been allowed to degenerate into a rigid objectivism, and a concern for reliable explanations of human behavior has been allowed to collapse into a dogmatic focus on constrained maximization. The feminist interpretation advanced in this book does not depend on a world view that sees current economic practitioners as individually malicious, or sees sexism behind every tree, or sees formalism as a source of pure evil. It does not argue for a feminine economics, or for a new economics to be practiced only by females. What it argues for is a change in the value system of economics, so that economics can become flexible as well as hard, contextual as well as logical, human as well as scientific, and rich as well as precise. Such an economics would be more adequate for analysis of the economic behavior of both women and men, and by both male and female practitioners.

As I write this, I have no great hopes of the discipline of economics doing an overnight turnaround. The pressures towards disciplinary conformity to the usual biases remain great. I see encouraging movements, however, in a number of areas. On the explicitly feminist side, the formation of the International Association for Feminist Economics as well as recent conferences and publications have given tremendous moral support to the sizable number of feminist economists who, until recently, were easily led to believe that each was only an isolated misfit. Continued feminist activities outside the profession persist in challenging the culture of sexism in general. On a less explicitly feminist side, many economists continue to ignore the value system of the profession as best they can – throwing away their graduate training and highest professional ambitions, if necessary – to include in their work the sort of rich and practical approaches that lead to actual accumulation of economic knowledge. For such economists, this book should be read not as a condemnation, but as encouragement; as a nudge to examine

150

one's work for remaining sexist biases; and as a call to be less shy about asserting standards of high quality research in one's roles as colleague, referee, and instructor. The economists of the future, of course, are the students of today. I hope this book will help to encourage perseverance among students who want to use their studies to the benefit of their fellow human beings, as well as help to provoke change among those responsible for the students' instruction.

BIBLIOGRAPHY

Aaron, Henry J. (1994) "Distinguished lecture on economics in government: public policy, values, and consciousness," *Journal of Economic Perspectives*, Spring, 8(2): 3–21.

Abel, Andrew B. and Bernanke, Ben S. (1992) *Macroeconomics*, New York: Addison-Wesley Publishing Co.

Adams, Douglas (1983) *Life, the Universe, and Everything*, New York: Pocket Books.

Akerlof, George A. and Yellen, Janet L. (1988) "Fairness and unemployment," *American Economic Review* 78(2): 44–9.

—— (1990) "The fair wage-effort hypothesis and unemployment," *Quarterly Journal of Economics* 105(20): 255–83.

Albelda, Randy (1992) "The impact of feminism on economics: what do economists think?", paper presented at the First Conference on Feminist Economics, Washington DC, July.

Alcoff, Linda (1988) "Cultural feminism versus post-structuralism: the identity crisis in feminist theory," *Signs* 13: 405–36.

Alcoff, Linda and Potter, Elizabeth (eds) (1993) *Feminist Epistemologies*, New York: Routledge.

Amariglio, Jack (1988) "The body, economic discourse and power: an economist's introduction to Foucault," *History of Political Economy* 20(4): 583–613.

American Economic Association (AEA) (1895) "Constitution," *Publications of the American Economic Association* 10: 10.

American Economic Association (1991) (untitled) *American Economic Review* 81, May: vi.

Antony, Louise M. and Witt, Charlotte (eds) (1993) *A Mind of One's Own: Feminist Essays on Reason and Objectivity*, Boulder: Westview Press.

Assarsson, Bengt (1985) "Prices and income distribution policy," paper presented at the World Congress of the Econometric Society, Cambridge, MA, USA, 17–24 August.

Atkinson, A.B. and Bourguignon, F. (1989) "The design of direct taxation and family benefits," *Journal of Public Economics* 41: 3–29.

Babcock, Barbara Allen, Freedman, Ann E., Norton, Eleanor Holmes and Ross, Susan C. (1975) *Sex Discrimination and the Law: Causes and Remedies*, Boston: Little, Brown and Company.

Baier, Annette C. (1987) "Hume, the women's moral theorist?" in Diana Meyers and Eva Feder Kittay (eds) *Women and Moral Theory*, Totowa NJ: Rowman and Littlefield.

BIBLIOGRAPHY

Bakker, Isabella (ed.) (1994) *The Strategic Silence: Gender and Economic Policy*, London: Zed Books.

Banks, James, Richard Blundell and Preston, Ian (1991) "Life-cycle expenditure allocations and the consumption costs of children," mimeo, Institute for Fiscal Studies.

Bannister, Robert C. (1987) *Sociology and Scientism: The American Quest for Objectivity, 1880–1940*, Chapel Hill: UNC Press.

Barten, Anton P. (1964) "Family composition, prices and expenditure patterns," in P.E. Hart, G. Mills, and J.K. Whitaker (eds) *Econometric Analysis for National Economic Planning*, London: Butterworth.

Becker, Gary S. (1974) "A theory of social interactions," *Journal of Political Economy* 82: 1063–93.

—— (1976) *The Economic Approach to Human Behavior*, Chicago: The University of Chicago Press.

—— (1981) *A Treatise on the Family*, Cambridge: Harvard University Press.

Belenky, Mary Field, Clinchy, Blythe McVicker Goldberger, Nancy Rule and Tarule, Jill Mattuck (1986) *Women's Ways of Knowing: The Development of Self, Voice, and Mind*, New York: Basic Books.

Bem, Sandra L. (1974) "The measurement of psychological androgyny," *Journal of Consulting and Clinical Psychology* 42(2): 155–62.

—— (1981) "Gender schema theory: a cognitive account of sex typing," *Psychological Review* 88(4): 354–64.

—— (1983) "Gender schema theory and its implications for child development: rising gender–a-schematic children in a gender-schematic society," *Signs* 8(4): 598–616.

Beneria, Lourdes (1992) "Accounting for women's work: the progress of two decades," *World Development* 20(11): 1547–60.

Benhabib, Seyla (1987) "The generalized and the concrete other: the Kohlberg–Gilligan controversy and moral theory," in Diana Meyers and Eva Feder Kittay (eds) *Women and Moral Theory*, Totowa NJ: Rowman and Littlefield.

—— (1990) "Epistemologies of Postmodernism: a rejoinder to Jean-François Lyotard, in Linda J. Nicholson (ed.) *Feminism/Postmodernism*, New York: Routledge.

Bergmann, Barbara R. (1986) *The Economic Emergence of Women*, New York: Basic Books.

—— (1987) "Measurement' or Finding Things Out in Economics," *Journal of Economic Education* 18(2): 191–203.

—— (1994) "Re: Housework," electronic posting to the FEMECON-L listserver, 7 July.

Bernard, Jessie (1987) "Reviewing the impact of women's studies on sociology," in Christie Farnham (ed.) *The Impact of Feminist Research in the Academy*, Bloomington: Indiana University Press.

Blackorby, Charles and Donaldson, David (1991) "Adult-equivalence scales and the economic implementation of interpersonal comparisons of well-being," Department of Economics, The University of British Columbia discussion paper no. 91–08 (Revision of No. 87–05, 1985).

Bleier, Ruth (1986) "Sex differences research: science or belief?", *Feminist Approaches to Science*, New York: Pergamon Press.

Blinder, Alan S. (1988) "The challenge of high unemployment," *American Economic Review*, May, 78(2): 1–15.

—— (1989) *Macroeconomics Under Debate*, New York: Harvester Wheatsheaf.

Blinder, Alan S. (1991) "Why are prices sticky? Preliminary results from an interview study," AEA Papers and Proceedings 81(2): 89–100.

Bloor, David [1976] (1991) *Knowledge and Social Imagery*, London: Routledge & Kegan Paul Ltd.

Blumberg, Rae Lesser (1988) "Income under female versus male control," *Journal of Family Issues* 9: 51–84.

Blundell, Richard W. (1980) "Estimating continuous consumer equivalence scales in an expenditure model with labor supply," *European Economic Review* 14: 145–57.

Blundell, Richard W. and Lewbel, Arthur (1991) "The information content of equivalence scales," *Journal of Econometrics* 50(1–2): 49–68.

Bojer, Hilde (1977) "The effect on consumption of household size and composition," *European Economic Review* 9: 169–93.

Bordo, Susan (1986) "The Cartesian masculinization of thought," *Signs: Journal of Women in Culture and Society* 11(3): 439–56.

—— (1987) *The Flight to Objectivity: Essays on Cartesianism and Culture*, Albany: State University of New York Press.

—— (1990) "Feminism, Postmodernism, and gender-skepticism," in Linda J. Nicholson (ed.) *Feminism/Postmodernism*, New York: Routledge.

Boulding, Kenneth E. (1969) "Economics vs. a moral science," *American Economic Review* 59(1): 1–12.

—— (1986) "What went wrong with economics," *American Economist* 30(1): 5–12.

Bourguignon, François (1989) "Family size and social utility: income distribution dominance criteria," *Journal of Econometrics* 42: 67–80.

Bourguignon, François and Chiappori, Pierre-André (1992) "Collective models of household behavior: an introduction," *European Economic Review* 36(2–3), April: 355–64.

Brazer, Harvey E. (1977) "Comments [on McIntyre and Oldman]," in J.A. Pechman (ed.) *Comprehensive Income Taxation*, Washington D.C.: Brookings.

—— (1980) "Income tax treatment of the family," in H.J. Aaron and M.J. Boskin (eds) *The Economics of Taxation*, Washington, D.C.: Brookings Institution.

Brown, J.A.C. (1964) "Discussion," in P.E. Hart, G. Mills, and J.K. Whitaker (eds), *Econometric Analysis for National Economic Planning*, London: Butterworth.

Buber, Martin (1958) *I and Thou*, New York: Scribner's.

Buhmann, Brigitte, Rainwater, Lee, Schmaus, Guenther and Smeeding, Timothy (1988) "Equivalence scales, well-being, inequality, and poverty: sensitivity estimates across ten countries using the Luxembourg Income Study (LIS) database," *Review of Income and Wealth*: 115–42.

Caldwell, Bruce J. and Coats, A.W. (1984) "The rhetoric of economists: a comment on McCloskey," *Journal of Economic Literature* 22: 575–8.

Chiappori, Pierre-André (1988) "Rational household labor supply," *Econometrica* 56(1): 63–89.

Chodorow, Nancy Julia (1978) *The Reproduction of Mothering: Psychoanalysis and the Sociology of Gender*, Berkeley: University of California Press.

—— (1980) "Gender, relation, and difference in psychoanalytic perspective," in Hester Eisenstein and Alice Jardine (eds) *The Future of Difference*, New Brunswick: Rutgers University Press.

Clark, J.M. (1919) "Economic theory in an era of social readjustment," *American Economic Review*, Supplement 9, March: 280–90.

Coats, A.W. (1960) "The first two decades of the American Economic Association," *American Economic Review* 50: 555–74.

—— (1984) "The sociology of knowledge and the history of economics," *Research in the History of Economic Thought and Methodology* 2: 211–34.

Cohen, Edwin (1983) "Commentary," in Rudolph G. Penner (ed) *Taxing the Family*, Washington DC: American Enterprise Institute.

Cooter, Robert and Rappoport, Peter 1984. "Were the ordinalists wrong about welfare economics?", *Journal of Economic Literature* 22: 507–30.

Corbett, Greville (1991) *Gender*, Cambridge: Cambridge University Press.

Crawford, Mary (1989) "Agreeing to differ: feminist epistemologies and women's ways of knowing," in Mary Crawford and Margaret Gentry (eds) *Gender and Thought: Psychological Perspectives*, New York: Springer-Verlag.

Daly, Herman E. and Cobb, John B. (1989) *For the Common Good: Redirecting the Economy Toward Community, the Environment, and a Sustainable Future*, Boston, MA: Beacon Press.

Davis, Philip J. and Hersh, Reuben (1987) "Rhetoric and mathematics," in John S. Nelson *et al.* (eds) *The Rhetoric of the Human Sciences*, Madison: University of Wisconsin Press.

Deaton, Angus S. and Muellbauer, John (1980) *Economics and Consumer Behavior*, Cambridge: Cambridge University Press.

—— (1986) "On measuring child costs: with applications to poor countries," *Journal of Political Economy* 94: 720–44.

Deaton, Angus S., Ruiz-Castillo, Javier and Thomas, Duncan (1989) "The influence of household composition on household expenditure patterns: theory and Spanish evidence," *Journal of Political Economy* 97: 179–200.

Debreu, Gerard (1991) "The mathematization of economic theory," *American Economic Review* 81: 1–7.

Del Boca, Daniela and Flinn, Christopher J. (1992) "Expenditure decisions of divorced mothers and income composition," C.V. Starr Center for Applied Economics Research Report No. 92–40. *Journal of Human Resources*, forthcoming.

Derrida, Jacques (1976) *Of Grammatology*, Baltimore: Johns Hopkins University Press.

Devine, Edward T. (1894) "The economic function of woman," *Annals of the American Academy of Political and Social Science* 5, November: 361–76.

DeWald, William G., Thursby, Jerry G. and Anderson, Richard G. (1986) "Replication in empirical economics: the *Journal of Money, Credit, and Banking* project," *American Economic Review* 76(4), September: 587–603.

Dimen, Muriel (1989) "Power, sexuality, & intimacy," in Alison M. Jaggar and Susan R. Bordo (eds) *Gender, Body, and Knowledge: Feminist Reconstruction of Being and Knowing*, New Brunswick: Rutgers University Press.

Dixon, Vernon J. (1970) "The di-unital approach to 'Black economics,'" *American Economic Review* 60(2): 424–9.

—— (1977) "African-oriented and Euro-American-oriented world views: research methodologies and economics," *Review of Black Political Economy* 7: 119–56.

Duesenberry, James S. (1960) "Comments," in National Bureau of Economic Research *Demographic and Economic Change in Developed Countries*: 231–4.

Dwyer, Daisy and Bruce, Judith (1988) *A Home Divided: Women and Income in the Third World*, Stanford: Stanford University Press.

Easlea, Brian (1980) *Witch Hunting, Magic and the New Philosophy: An Introduction to Debates of the Scientific Revolution*, Atlantic Highlands NJ.: Humanities Press.

Easlea, Brian (1986) "The masculine image of science with special reference to physics: how much does gender really matter?" in Jan Harding (ed.) *Perspectives on Gender & Science*, London: The Falmer Press.

Edwards, Carolyn S., Marr, Janet S. and Gray, Bruce C. (1982) "The development of the USDA estimates of the cost of raising a child," *Social Indicators Research* 10: 227–71.

Eisenstein, Hester and Jardine, Alice (eds) (1985) *The Future of Difference*, New Brunswick: Rutgers University Press.

Elliot, Patricia (1994) "More thinking about gender: a response to Julie A. Nelson," *Hypatia: A Journal of Feminist Philosophy* 9(1): 195–8.

Elshtain, Jean Bethke (1987) "Feminist political rhetoric and women's studies," in John S. Nelson, Allan McGill, and Donald N. McCloskey (eds) *The Rhetoric of the Human Sciences*, Madison: University of Wisconsin Press.

Ely, Richard T. (1892) "The higher education of women: in the School of Economics, Political Science, and History of the University of Wisconsin," *The Christian Union* [in Ely personal papers archived at the University of Wisconsin].

—— (1936) "The founding and early history of the American Economic Association," *American Economic Review* 26(1): 141–50.

—— (1938) (reprinted 1977) *Ground Under Our Feet: An Autobiography*, New York: Macmillan.

Engel, Ernst (1857) "Die Productions und Consumtionsverhaltnisse des Konigsreichs Sachsen," Zeitscrift des Statistischen Bureaus des Koniglich Sachischen Ministeriums des Innern 3.

—— (1895) "Die Libenskosten Belgischer Arbieter-familien Fruher und Jetzt," *Bulletin de L'Institut International de Statistique* 9: 1–124.

England, Paula (1992) *Comparable Worth: Theories and Evidence*, New York: Aldine De Gruyter.

—— 1993. "The separative self: androcentric bias in neoclassical assumptions," in M.A. Ferber and J.A. Nelson (eds) *Beyond Economic Man*, Chicago: University of Chicago Press.

Espenshade, Thomas J. (1984) *Investing in Children: New Estimates of Parental Expenditures*, Washington DC: The Urban Institute Press.

Federal Register, (1994) 59, (28), 10 February: 6277.

Fee, Elizabeth (1983) "Women's nature and scientific objectivity," in Marian Lowe and Ruth Hubbard (eds) *Women's Nature: Rationalizations of Inequality*, New York: Pergamon Press.

Ferber, Marianne A. (1990) "Gender and the study of economics," in Phillip Saunders and William Walstad (eds) *The Principles of Economics Course: A Handbook for Instructors*, New York: McGraw-Hill.

Ferber, Marianne A. and Birnbaum, Bonnie G. (1977) "The 'New Home Economics:' retrospects and prospects," *Journal of Consumer Research* 4: 19–28.

—— (1980) "Economics of the family: who maximizes what?" *Family Economics Review*: 13–16.

Ferber, Marianne A. and Nelson, Julie A. (eds) (1993) *Beyond Economic Man: Feminist Theory and Economics*, Chicago: University of Chicago Press.

Feyerabend, Paul (1975) *Against Method*, New York: Humanities Press.

Fischer, Gordon (1991) personal communication, United States Department of Health and Human Services.

Fisher, Franklin M. (1987) "Household equivalence scales and interpersonal comparisons," *Review of Economic Studies* 54: 519–24.

Flax, Jane (1990) "Postmodernism and gender relations in feminist theory," in Linda J. Nicholson (ed.) *Feminism/Postmodernism*, New York: Routledge.

Folbre, Nancy (1988) "The black four of hearts: toward a new paradigm of household economics," in Daisy Dwyer and Judith Bruce (eds) *A Home Divided: Women and Income in the Third World*, Stanford: Stanford University Press.

—— (1991) "The unproductive housewife: her evolution in nineteenth-century economic thought," *Signs: Journal of Women in Culture and Society* 16(3): 463–84.

—— (1993a) "'Guys don't do that': gender groups and social norms," mimeo, University of Massachusetts.

—— (1993b) "Socialism, feminist and scientific," in M.A. Ferber and J.A. Nelson (eds) *Beyond Economic Man*, Chicago: University of Chicago Press.

—— (1994) *Who Pays for the Kids? Gender and the Structures of Constraint*, New York: Routledge.

—— (1994) "Domesticate the gross product," *Dollars and Sense*, March/April: 7.

Folbre, Nancy and Heidi Hartmann (1988) "The rhetoric of self-interest: ideology and gender in economic theory," in Arjo Klamer, Donald N. McCloskey, and Robert M. Solow (eds) *The Consequences of Economic Rhetoric*, Cambridge: Cambridge University Press.

Foucault, Michel (1976) *The Archaeology of Knowledge*, New York: Harper & Row.

Frank, Francine Wattman and Treichler, Paula A. (1989) *Language, Gender and Professional Writing: Theoretical Approaches and Guidelines for Nonsexist Usage*, New York: The Modern Language Association of America.

Frank, Robert H. (1988) *Passions Within Reason: The Strategic Role of the Emotions*, New York: W.W. Norton & Co.

Frank, Robert H., Gilovish, Thomas and Regan, Dennis T. (1993) "Does studying economics inhibit cooperation?" *Journal of Economic Perpectives* 7(2): 159–71.

Fraser, Nancy and Nicholson, Linda J. (1990) "Social criticism without philosophy: an encounter between feminism and postmodernism," in Linda J. Nicholson (ed.) *Feminism/Postmodernism*, New York: Routledge.

Frisch, Ragnar (1933) "Editorial," *Econometrica* 1: 1–4.

Furner, Mary O. (1975) *Advocacy & Objectivity: A Crisis in the Professionalization of American Social Science, 1865–1905*, Lexington: The University Press of Kentucky.

Galbraith, John Kenneth (1973) "Power and the useful economist," *American Economic Review*, March, 63(1): 1–11.

Georgescu-Roegen, Nicholas (1966) *Analytical Economics*, Cambridge: Harvard University Press.

—— (1971) *The Entropy Law and the Economic Process*, Cambridge: Harvard University Press.

Gergen, Kenneth J. (1985) "The social constructionist movement in modern psychology," *American Psychologist* 40: 266–75.

Gilligan, Carol (1982) *In A Difference Voice: Psychological Theory and Women's Development*, Cambridge: Harvard University Press.

—— (1986) "Reply," *Signs* 11: 324–33.

—— (1987a) "Moral orientation and moral development," in D. Meyers and E.F. Kittay (eds) *Women and Moral Theory*, Totowa NJ: Rowman and Littlefield.

—— (1987b) "Remapping development: the power of divergent data," in

Christie Farnham (ed.) *The Impact of Feminist Research in the Academy*, Bloomington: Indiana University Press.

Gordon, Robert Aaron (1976) "Rigor and relevance in a changing institutional setting," *The American Economic Review*, March, 66(1): 1–14.

Gorman, W.M. (1976) "Tricks with utility functions," in J.H. Artis and A.R. Nobay (eds) *Essays in Economic Analysis*, Cambridge: Cambridge University Press.

Grapard, Ulla (1992 "Who can see the invisible hand? Or, from the benevolence of the butcher's wife," paper presented at the First Conference on Feminist Economics, Washington D.C., 24–26 June.

Grassi, Ernesto (1980) *Rhetoric as Philosophy: The Humanist Tradition*, University Park: The Pennsylvania State University Press.

Gronau, Reuben (1988) "Consumption technology and the intrafamily distribution of resources: adult equivalence scales reexamined," *Journal of Political Economy* 96: 1183–1205.

—— (1991) "The intra-family allocation of goods: how to separate the adult from the child," *Journal of Labor Economics* 9: 207–35.

Gwartney, James D., Stroup, Richard and Clark, J.R. (1985) *Essentials of Economics*, New York: Academic Press.

Haddad, Lawrence and Kanbur, Ravi (1990) "How serious is the neglect of intrahousehold inequality," *Economic Journal* 100: 866–81.

Hammond, Claire H. (1993) "American women and the professionalization of economics," *Review of Social Economy* 51(3): 347–70.

Hampton, Jean (1993) "Selflessness and the loss of self," *Social Philosophy & Policy* 10(1): 135–65.

Haraway, Donna J. (1991) *Simians, Cyborgs, and Women: The Reinvention of Nature*, New York: Routledge.

Harding, Jan (ed) (1986) *Perspectives on Gender and Science*, London: The Falmer Press.

Harding, Sandra (1986) *The Science Question in Feminism*, Ithaca: Cornell University Press.

—— (1987) "The curious coincidence of feminine and African moralities: challenges for feminist theory," in Diana Meyers and Eva Feder Kittay (eds) *Women and Moral Theory*, Totowa NJ: Rowman and Littlefield.

—— (1991) *Whose Science? Whose Knowledge? Thinking from Women's Lives*, Ithaca: Cornell University Press.

—— (1993a) "Feminist philosophy of science: the objectivity question," paper presented at the conference "Out of the Margin: Feminist Perspectives on Economic Theory", Amsterdam, 2–3 June.

—— (1993b) "Rethinking standpoints epistemology: 'what is strong objectivity?'" in Linda Alcoff and Elizabeth Potter (eds) *Feminist Epistemologies*, New York: Routledge.

Harding, Sandra and O'Barr, Jean F. (eds) (1987) *Sex and Scientific Inquiry*, Chicago: The University of Chicago Press.

Hare-Mustin, Rachel T. and Marecek, Jeanne (1988) "The meaning of difference: gender theory, postmodernism, and psychology," *American Psychologist* 43(6): 455–64.

Harrington, Joseph (1989) "Cooperation among randomly meeting agents under imperfect information," mimeo, Johns Hopkins University, Department of Economics, August.

Hartsock, Nancy (1983) *Money, Sex and Power: Toward a Feminist Historical Materialism*, New York: Longman.

—— (1990) "Foucault on power: a theory for women?" in Linda J. Nicholson (ed.) *Feminism/Postmodernism*, New York: Routledge.

Heilbroner, Robert L. (1986) *The Worldly Philosophers: The Lives, Times and Ideas of the Great Economic Thinkers*, New York: Simon & Schuster, Inc.

Henderson, A.M. (1950) "The cost of a family," *Review of Economic Studies* 17: 127–48.

Hewitson, Gillian (1993) "Deconstructing Robinson Crusoe: the role of binary oppositions in economics," paper presented at the conference "Out of the Margin: Feminist Perspectives on Economic Theory," Amsterdam, 2–5 June.

Hillman, James (1972) *The Myth of Analysis*, New York: Harper & Row.

Hobbes, Thomas (1966) "Philosophical rudiments concerning government and society," *The English Works of Thomas Hobbes*. Darmstadt, Sir W. Molesworth (ed.) (cited in Seyla Benhabib, 1987).

Hobbes, Thomas (1951, 1984) *Leviathan* (C.M. MacPherson (ed.), New York: Penguin [reprinted from the 1651 edition, chapter V].

Hochschild, Arlie Russell (1989) *The Second Shift: Working Parents and the Revolution at Home*, New York: Viking Press.

hooks, bell (1990) *Yearning: Race, Gender, and Cultural Politics*, Boston: South End Press.

Huston, Aletha C. (1983) "Sex-typing," in P.H. Mussen and E. M. Hetherington (eds) *Handbook of Child Psychology* [*Vol. 4*] *Socialization, Personality and Social Development*, 4th edn, New York: Wiley.

Jennings, Ann L. (1993) "Public or private? Institutional economics and feminism," in Marianne A. Ferber and Julie A. Nelson (eds) *Beyond Economic Man*, Chicago: University of Chicago Press.

Jevons, W. Stanley (1924) *The Theory of Political Economy*, 4th edn [cited in Georgescu-Roegen 1972: 40].

Johnson, Mark (1987) *The Body in the Mind: The Bodily Basis of Meaning, Imagination, and Reason*, Chicago: University of Chicago Press.

Jorgenson, Dale W. and Slesnick, Daniel T. (1987) "Aggregate consumer behavior and household equivalence scales," *Journal of Business & Economic Statistics* 5: 219–32.

Kahneman, Daniel, Knetsch, Jack L. and Thaler, Richard (1986) "Fairness as a constraint on profit seeking: entitlements in the market," *American Economic Review* 76(4): 728–41.

Kakwani, Nanak C. (1980) *Income Inequality and Poverty: Methods of Estimation and Policy Applications*, New York: Oxford University Press.

Kapteyn, Arie and van Praag, B.M.S. (1976) "A new approach to the construction of family equivalence scales," *European Economic Review* 7: 313–35.

Kapteyn, Arie Kooreman, Peter and Willemse, Bob (1988) "Some methodological issues in the implementation of subjective poverty definitions," *Journal of Human Resources* 23: 222–42.

Keller, Catherine (1986) *From A Broken Web: Separation, Sexism, and Self*, Boston: Beacon Press.

Keller, Evelyn Fox (1983) *A Feeling for the Organism: The Life and Work of Barbara McClintock*, New York: Freeman.

—— (1985) *Reflection on Gender and Science*, New Haven, Conn: Yale University Press.

—— (1986a) "How gender matters: or, why it's so hard for us to count past two," in Jan Harding (ed.) *Perspectives on Gender & Science*, London: The Falmer Press.

Keller, Evelyn Fox (1986b) "Making gender visible in the pursuit of nature's secrets," in Teresa de Lauretis (ed.) *Feminist Studies/Critical Studies*, Bloomington: Indiana University Press.

—— (1987) "The gender/science system: or, is sex to gender as nature is to science?" *Hypatia* 2(3): 37–49.

Klamer, Arjo (1989) "On interpretive and feminist economics," presented at the annual meetings of the Southern Economic Association, November.

Knorr-Cetina, Karin (1991) "Epistemic cultures: forms of reason in science," *History of Political Economy* 23: 105–22.

Kuhn, Thomas (1962, 2nd edn 1970) *The Structure of Scientific Revolutions*, Chicago: University of Chicago Press.

Lakatos, Imre (1971) "History of science and its rational reconstructions," *Boston Studies 8*, eds R.C. Buck and R.S. Cohen.

Lakoff, George and Johnson, Mark (1980) *Metaphors We Live By*, Chicago: The University of Chicago Press.

Lange, Lynda (1983) "Woman is not a rational animal: on Aristotle's biology of reproduction," in Sandra Harding and Merril B. Hintikka (eds) *Discovering Reality*, Boston: D. Reidel Publishing Co.

Laslett, Barbara (1990) "Unfeeling knowledge: emotion and objectivity in the history of sociology," *Sociological Forum* 5: 413–33.

Lazear, Edward P. and Robert T. Michael (1980) "Family size and the distribution of real per capita income," *American Economic Review* 70, March: 91–107.

—— (1988) *Allocation of Income Within the Household*, Chicago: University of Chicago Press.

Leamer, Edward (1983) "Let's take the con out of econometrics," *American Economic Review* 73, March: 31–4.

Leontief, Wassily (1971) "Theoretical assumptions and nonobserved facts," *American Economic Review* 61: 1–7.

Levin, Lee B. (1995) "Toward a feminist, post-Keynesian theory of investment: a consideration of the socially- and emotionally-constituted nature of agent knowledge," in Edith Kuiper *et al.* (eds) *Out of the Margin: Feminist Perspectives on Economic Theory*, London: Routledge.

Lewbel, Arthur (1989) "Household equivalence scales and welfare comparisons," *Journal of Public Economics* 39: 377–91.

Lewin ICF (1990) *Estimates of Expenditures on Children and Child Support Guidelines*, report submitted to the Office of the Assistant Secretary for Planning and Evaluation, U.S. Department of Health and Human Services.

Lindert, Peter (1978) *Fertility and Scarcity in America*, Princeton: Princeton University Press.

Lloyd, Genevieve (1984) *The Man of Reason: 'Male' and 'Female' in Western Philosophy*, Minneapolis: University of Minnesota Press.

Longino, Helen (1990) *Science as Social Knowledge: Values and Objectivity in Scientific Inquiry*, Princeton: Princeton University Press.

Lucas, Robert E., Jr (1987) *Models of Business Cycles*, Oxford: Basil Blackwell.

Lundberg, Shelly and Pollak, Robert A. (1993) "Separate spheres bargaining and the marriage market," *Journal of Political Economy* 100(6): 988–1010.

Lundberg, Shelly and Pollak, Robert A. (1994) "Noncooperative bargaining models of marriage," *American Economic Review* 84(2): 132–7.

Lutz, Mark A. and Lux, Kenneth (1988) *Humanistic Economics: The New Challenge*, New York: The Bootstrap Press.

—— (1995) "Commenting on gendered economics: mushroom men, straw men and real persons," *Review of Social Economy* 53(1).

160

McCloskey, Donald N. (1985) *The Rhetoric of Economics*, Madison: University of Wisconsin Press.

—— (1988) "Some consequences of a feminine economics," mimeo, Project on the Rhetoric of Inquiry, December 1989, version presented at the annual meetings of the American Economic Association.

—— (1991) "Economic science: a search through the hyperspace of assumptions?" *Methodus: Bulletin of the International Network for Economic Method* 3: 6–16.

—— (1993) "Some consequences of a conjective economics," in Marianne A. Ferber and Julie A. Nelson (eds) *Beyond Economic Man: Feminist Theory and Economics*, Chicago: University of Chicago Press.

McCrate, Elaine (1987) "Trade, merger and employment: economic theory on marriage," *Review of Radical Political Economics* 19(1): 73–89.

McElroy, Marjorie B. (1990) "The empirical content of Nash-bargained household behavior," *Journal of Human Resources* 25: 4–583.

McElroy, Marjorie B. and Horney, Mary Jean (1981) "Nash bargained household decisions: towards a generalization of the theory of demand," *International Economic Review* 22: 333–49.

Maccoby, Eleanor E. and Masters, John C. (1970) "Attachment and dependency," in Paul H. Mussen (ed.) *Carmichael's Manual of Child Psychology (Vol. 2)*, New York: Wiley.

Mankiw, N. Gregory (1994) *Macroeconomics*, 2nd edn, New York: Worth Publishers.

Mansbridge, Jane (1993) "Feminism and democratic community," in John W. Chapman and Ian Shapiro (eds) *Democratic Community: NOMOS XXXV*, New York: New York University Press.

Manser, Marilyn and Brown, Murray (1980) "Marriage and household decision-making: a bargaining analysis," *International Economic Review* 21: 31–44.

Marcuss, Rosemary D. and Nielsen, Rosemarie N. (1985) "Women and families as taxpayers: a history," mimeo, Washington DC: The Women's Research and Education Institute, Presented at the conference "Federal Tax Policy: What's in it for Women and Families," March).

Margolis, Howard (1982) *Selfishness, Altruism and Rationality: A Theory of Social Choice*, Chicago: The University of Chicago Press.

—— (1987) *Patterns, Thinking, and Cognition: A Theory of Judgment*, Chicago: The University of Chicago Press.

Martin, Emily (1991) "The egg and the sperm: how science has constructed a romance based on stereotypical male–female roles," *Signs: Journal of Women in Culture and Society* 16: 485–501.

Mayer, Thomas (1993) *Truth vs. Precision in Economics*, Brookfield VT: Edward Elgar.

Mehta, Judith (1993) "Meaning in the context of bargaining games – narratives in opposition," in Willie Henderson *et al.*, (eds) *Economics and Language*, New York: Routledge.

Merchant, Carolyn (1980) *The Death of Nature: Women, Ecology and the Scientific Revolution*, San Francisco: Harper & Row.

Minarik, Joseph J. (1983) "Commentary," in Rudolph G. Penner (ed.) *Taxing the Family*, Washington, DC: American Enterprise Institute.

Mirowski, Philip (1988) *Against Mechanism: Protecting Economics from Science*, Totowa NJ: Rowman & Littlefield.

Morawski, J.G. (1987) "The troubled quest for masculinity, femininity and androgyny," *Review of Personality and Social Psychology* 7: 7–69.

Muellbauer, John (1974) "Household composition, Engel curves and welfare comparisons between households: a duality approach," *European Economic Review* 5: 103–22.

—— (1977) "Testing the Barten model of household composition effects and the cost of children," *Economics Journal* 87(9): 460–87.

—— (1980) "The estimation of the Prais–Houthakker model of equivalence scales," *Econometrica* 48(1): 153–76.

Munnell, Alicia H. (1980) "The couple versus the individual under the federal personal income tax," in Henry J. Aaron and Michael J. Boskin (eds) *The Economics of Taxation*, Washington, DC: The Brookings Institution.

Nelson, Julie A. (1988) "Household economies of scale in consumption: theory and evidence," *Econometrica* 56: 1301–14.

—— (1989) "Individual consumption within the household: a study of expenditures on clothing," *Journal of Consumer Affairs* 23, Summer: 21–44.

—— (1991) "'Independent of a base' equivalence scales estimation using United States micro-level data," Working Paper no. 392, Davis: University of California, Davis, Department of Economics.

—— (1992) "Methods of estimating household equivalence scales: an empirical investigation," *Review of Income and Wealth* 38(3): 295–310.

—— (1993a) "'Independent of a base' equivalence scales estimation using United States micro-level data," *Annales d'Economie et de Statistiques* 29: 43–63.

—— (1993b) "The study of choice or the study of provisioning? Gender and the definition of economics," in Marianne A. Ferber and Julie A. Nelson (eds) *Beyond Economic Man*, Chicago: University of Chicago Press.

Newlon, Daniel (1992) personal correspondence, 19 August.

Nicholson, Linda J. (ed.) (1990) *Feminism/Postmodernism*, London: Routledge.

Nussbaum, Martha C. (1992) "Human functioning and social justice: in defense of Aristotelian essentialism," *Political Theory* 20(2): 202–46.

—— (1993) "Emotions and women's capabilities," in Martha Nussbaum and Jonathan Glover (eds) *Women, Culture, and Development*, Oxford: Clarendon Press.

Nussbaum, Martha C. and Sen, Amartya (eds) (1993) *The Quality of Life*, Oxford: Clarendon Press.

Offen, Karen (1988) "Defining feminism: a comparative historical approach," *Signs* 14(1): 119–57.

Okin, Susan Moller (1989) *Gender, Justice, and the Family*, New York: Basic Books.

O'Neill, June (1983) "Family issues in taxation," in Rudolph G. Penner (ed.) *Taxing the Family*, Washington, DC: American Enterprise Institute.

Orshansky, Mollie (1965) "Counting the poor: another look at the poverty profile," *Social Security Bulletin*: 3–29.

Ortony, Andrew (ed.) (1979) "Metaphor: a multidimensional problem," *Metaphor and Thought*, Cambridge: Cambridge University Press.

Ott, Notburga (1995) "Fertility and division of work in the family: a game theoretic model of household decisions," in Edith Kuiper *et al.* (eds) *Out of the Margin: Feminist Perspectives on Economic Theory*, London: Routledge.

Pahl, Jan (1989) *Money and Marriage*, London: Macmillan Education Ltd.

Pechman, Joseph A. (1987) *Federal Tax Policy*, 5th edn, Washington, DC: Brookings Institution.

Pechman, Joseph A. and Engelhardt, Gary V. (1990) "The income tax treatment of the family: an international perspective," *National Tax Journal* 43(1): 1–22.

162

Phipps, Shelly A. (1991) "Price-sensitive adult-equivalence scales for Canada," mimeo, Department of Economics, Dalhousie University.

Piercy, Marge (1976) *Woman on the Edge of Time*, New York: Random House.

Plumwood, Val (1993) *Feminism and the Mastery of Nature*, Routledge, London.

Polachek, Solomon W. (1995) "Human capital and the gender earnings gap: a response to feminist critiques," in Edith Kuiper *et al.* (eds) *Out of the Margin: Feminist Perspectives on Economic Theory*, London: Routledge.

Pollak, Robert A. (1985) "A transaction cost approach to families and households," *Journal of Economic Literature* 23: 581–608.

—— (1991) "Welfare comparisons and situations comparisons," *Journal of Econometrics* 50: 31–48.

Pollak, Robert A. and Wales, Terence J. (1979) "Welfare comparisons and equivalence scales," *American Economic Review* 69: 216–21.

Poovey, Mary (1988) "Feminism and deconstruction," *Feminist Studies* 14: 51–65.

Potter, Elizabeth (1988, reprinted 1989) "Modeling the gender politics in science," *Hypatia* 3. Reprinted in Nancy Tuana (ed.) *Feminism and Science*, Bloomington: Indiana University Press.

Prais, S. J. and Houthakker, H.S. (1955) *The Analysis of Family Budgets*, Cambridge: Cambridge University Press.

Pujol, Michèle A. (1992) *Feminism and Anti-Feminism in Early Economic Thought*, Brookfield VT: Edward Elgar.

Rader, Benjamin G. (1966) *The Academic Mind and Reform: The Influence of Richard T. Ely in American Life*, Lexington: University of Kentucky Press.

Ray, Ranjan (1983) "Measuring the cost of children: an alternative approach." *Journal of Public Economics* 22: 89–102.

—— (1986) "Demographic variables and equivalence scales in a flexible demand system: the case of AIDS," *Applied Economics* 18: 265–87.

Renwick, Trudi J. and Bergmann, Barbara R. (1993) "A budget-based definition of poverty: with an application to single-parent families," *Journal of Human Resources*, Winter, 28(1): 1–24.

Ringen, Stein (1991) "Households, standard of living, and inequality," *Review of Income and Wealth* 37: 1–13.

Robbins, Lionel [1935] (1952) *An Essay on the Nature and Significance of Economic Science*, London: Macmillan.

Roos, Charles F. (1933) "The organization of the Econometric Society in Cleveland, Ohio, December 1930," *Econometrica* 1: 71–2.

Rorty, Richard (1979) *Philosophy and the Mirror of Nature*, Princeton: Princeton University Press.

—— (1989) *Contingency, Irony, and Solidarity*, Cambridge: Cambridge University Press.

Rosetti, Jane (1993) "The ambiguous benefits of postmodernism for feminist economics," paper prepared for presentation at the 1993 Allied Social Sciences Association meetings, Anaheim, California (xerox, Economics Department, Franklin and Marshall College.)

Rossiter, Margaret (1982) *Women Scientists in America: Struggles and Strategies to 1940*, Baltimore: Johns Hopkins University Press.

Rothbarth, Erwin (1943) "Note on a method of determining equivalent income for families of different composition," App. 4 in *War-Time Pattern of Saving and Spending*, Charles Madge, Occasional Paper no. 4. Cambridge: Cambridge University Press (for Nat. Inst. Econ. and Soc. Res.).

Rothman, Gerald C. (1985) *Philanthropists, Therapists, and Activists: A Century of*

Ideological Conflict in Social Work, Cambridge MA: Schenkman Publishing Company.

Ruddick, Sara (1987) "Remarks on the sexual politics of reason," in Diana Meyers and Eva Feder Kittay (eds) *Women and Moral Theory*, Totowa NJ: Rowman and Littlefield.

—— (1989) *Maternal Thinking: Towards a Politics of Peace*, Boston: Beacon Press.

Ruttenberg, Ruth and McCarthy, Amy (1984) "Women and tax policy," mimeo, Washington, DC: The Women's Research and Education Institute, presented at the National Conference on Women, the Economy and Public Policy, Washington, DC, June.

Samuelson, Paul A. (1956) "Social indifference curves," *The Quarterly Journal of Economics* 70(1): 1–22.

Sass, Steven A. (1988) "An uneasy relationship: the business community and academic economists at the University of Pennsylvania," in W.J. Barber (ed.) *Breaking the Academic Mold: Economists and American Higher Learning in the Nineteenth Century*, Middletown Connecticut: Wesleyan University Press.

Sawhill, Isabel V. (1977) "Economic perspectives on the family," *Daedalus* 106: 115–25.

Schabas, Margaret (1993) "What's so wrong with physics envy?" in Neil de Marchi (ed.) *Non-Natural Social Science*, annual supplement to Volume 25 of the *History of Political Economy*, Durham: Duke University Press.

Schiebinger, Londa (1987) "The history and philosophy of women in science: a review essay," *Signs: Journal of Women in Culture and Society* 12: 305–32.

Schumpeter, Joseph (1933) "The common sense of econometrics," *Econometrica* 1: 5–12.

Scott, Joan W. (1988) "Deconstructing equality-versus-difference: or, the uses of poststructuralist theory for feminism," *Feminist Studies* 14: 33–50.

Seiz, Janet A. (1991) "The bargaining approach and feminist methodology," *Review of Radical Political Economics* 23(1&2): 22–9.

Sen, Amartya (1982) *Choice, Welfare and Measurement*, Cambridge: The MIT Press.

—— (1984) *Resources, Values, and Development*, Cambridge: Harvard University Press, chapter 15.

—— 1985. "Women, technology, and sexual divisions," in United Nations Conference on Trade and Development, *Trade and Development: An UNCTAD Review* 6: 195–223.

—— (1987) *The Standard of Living*, Cambridge: Cambridge University Press.

—— (1990) "Gender and cooperative conflicts," in Irene Tinker (ed.) *Persistent Inequalities*, Oxford: Oxford University Press.

—— (1992) *Objectivity and Position*, The Lindley Lecture, University of Kansas, 5 March.

—— (1993) "Capability and well-being," in Martha C. Nussbaum and Amartya Sen (eds) *The Quality of Life*, Oxford: Clarendon Press.

Seneca, Joseph J. and Taussig, Michael K. (1971) "Family equivalence scales and personal income tax exemptions for children," *Review of Economics and Statistics* 53: 253–62.

Solow, Robert M. (1990) *The Labor Market as a Social Institution*, Cambridge MA: Basil Blackwell.

Stern, Karl (1965) *The Flight from Women*, New York: The Noonday Press.

Stiglitz, Joseph E. (1988) *Economics of the Public Sector*, 2nd edn, New York: W.W. Norton & Company.

Strassmann, Diana L. (1993a) "The stories of economics and the power of the storyteller," *History of Political Economy* 25(1): 147–65.

—— (1993b) "Not a free market: the rhetoric of disciplinary authority in economics" in Marianne A. Ferber and Julie A. Nelson (eds) *Beyond Economic Man*, Chicago: University of Chicago Press.

Strober, Myra (1987) "The scope of microeconomics: implications for economic education," *Journal of Economic Education* 18: 135–49.

Summers, Lawrence H. (1991) "The scientific illusion in empirical macroeconomics," *Scandinavian Journal of Economics* 93(1): 129–48.

Sydenstricker, Edgar and King, Willford I. (1921) "The measurement of the relative economic status of families," *Quarterly Publication of the American Statistical Association* 17: 842–57.

Tauchen, Helen V., Witte, Ann Dryden and Long, Sharon K. (1991) "Domestic violence: a nonrandom affair," *International Economic Review* 32: 491–511.

Thomas, Duncan (1990) "Intra-household resource allocation: an inferential approach," *Journal of Human Resources* 25: 635–64.

Thomson, Dorothy Lampen (1973) *Adam Smith's Daughters*, New York: Exposition Press.

Thurow, Lester C. (1988) "Producer economics," *Proceedings of the Forty-First Annual Meeting of the Industrial Relations Research Association*: 9–20.

Tobin, James (1985) "Neoclassical theory in America: J.B. Clark and Fisher," *American Economic Review* 75, December: 28–38.

Tuana, Nancy (ed.)(1989) *Feminism & Science*, Bloomington: Indiana University Press.

Turchi, Boone A. (1975) *The Demand for Children: The Economics of Fertility in the United States*, Cambridge: Ballinger Publishing Co.

United Nations Development Program (1990) *Human Development Report 1990*, New York: Oxford University Press.

United States Department of Commerce (1993) *Current Population Reports*, Series P-60, No. 186-RD "Measuring the Effects of Benefits and Taxes on Income and Poverty: 1992" (September), Washington, DC: U.S. Government Printing Office.

United States Department of Labor, Bureau of Labor Statistics (1960) "Estimating equivalent incomes or budget costs by family type," *Monthly Labor Review* (November): 1197–1200.

United States Department of Labor, Bureau of Labor Statistics (1948) "Workers' budgets in the United States: city families and single persons, 1946 and 1947," Bulletin No. 927: 49–51.

United States Department of Labor, Bureau of Labor Statistics (1968) "Revised equivalence scale: for estimating equivalent incomes or budget costs by family type," Bulletin No. 1570–2.

United States Department of Treasury (1993) *1040: Forms and Instructions*.

United States House of Representatives, Committee on Ways and Means (1985) *Children in Poverty*. Committee Print, 22 May.

van der Gaag, Jacques (1982) "On measuring the cost of children," *Children and Youth Services Review* 4: 104.

van der Gaag, Jacques, and Smolensky, Eugene (1982) "True household equivalence scales and characteristics of the poor in the United States," *Review of Income and Wealth* 28: 17–28.

Varian, Hal R. (1984) *Microeconomic Analysis*, New York: W.W. Norton & Company.

Vickery, Clair (1977) "The time-poor: a new look at poverty," *Journal of Human Resources* 12: 27–48.

Waring, Marilyn (1988) *If Women Counted: A New Feminist Economics*, New York: Harper & Row.

Watts, Harold W. (1967) "The iso-prop index: an approach to the determination of differential poverty income thresholds," *Journal of Human Resources* 2: 3–18.

Webster's New Collegiate Dictionary (1974) Springfield: G & C Merriam Co.

Weinreich-Haste, Helen (1986) "Brother sun, sister moon: does rationality overcome a dualistic world view?" in Jan Harding (ed.) *Perspectives on Gender & Science*, London: The Falmer Press.

West, Robin (1988) "Jurisprudence and gender," *The University of Chicago Law Review* 55(1): 1–72.

Whitehead, Alfred North (1925) *Science and the Modern World*, New York: The Macmillan Company.

Williams, Faith M. and Hanson, Alice C. (1940) "Money disbursements of wage earners and clerical workers," U.S. Department of Labor, Bureau of Labor Statistics Bulletin 636: 23–9.

Williams, Rhonda M (1993) "Race, deconstruction, and the emergent agenda of feminist economic theory," in M.A. Ferber and J.A. Nelson, (eds) *Beyond Economic Man*, Chicago: University of Chicago Press.

Williams, Wendy Webster (1978) *Sex Discrimination and the Law: Causes and Remedies, 1978 Supplement*, Boston: Little, Brown and Co.

Wilshire, Donna (1989) "The use of myth, image, and the female body in revisioning knowledge," in Alison M. Jagger and Susan R. Bordo, (eds) *Gender/Body/Knowledge: Feminist Reconstructions of Being and Knowing*, New Brunswick: Rutgers University Press.

Zelizer, Viviana A. (1994) "The creation of domestic currencies," *American Economic Review* 84(2): 138–42.

INDEX